The Gypsies of Spain

Text by
Jan Yoors
Photographs by
André A. López

Macmillan Publishing Co., Inc.
NEW YORK

397
Y8g

In memory of Pedro Closa, S.J.
the Pedro in these pages,
who, I learned
as this book went to press,
died a violent
and untimely death
because of his love
for the Gypsies of Spain.

—Jan Yoors

For Nanushka,
without whose love and strength
this work would not exist.
Thank you.

—André A. López

Contents

¡Oh, ciudad de los Gitanos!
La Guardia Civil se aleja
por un túnel de silencio
mientras las llamas te cercan.

¡Oh, ciudad de los Gitanos!
¿Quien te vió y no te recuerda?
Que te busquen en mi frente.
Juego de la luna y de arena.

— Federico García Lorca

Oh, city of Gypsies!
The Civil Guard rides away
through a tunnel of silence
while around you are flames.

Oh, city of Gypsies!
Who could see you and forget?
Let them seek you on my brow.
The play of the moon and sand.

Foreword

IN an early spring day in 1934 I left my parents' home in Antwerp, Belgium, to join a band of nomadic Gypsies passing through. I was twelve years old. I did not leave home because I was unhappy there nor was I in any way rebellious but because I wanted to better know the wonderful people my father often spoke about with affection and longing. I went to play with the Gypsy children at their encampment. I "overstayed" for about six months. When I returned home my parents received me with open arms. During the next six years I was torn between two worlds and managed to spend time in both. A Gypsy called Pulika adopted me under dramatic circumstances. I learned to speak Romani and strongly identified with the Gypsies. With them I wandered throughout western Europe and the Balkans. I wrote about these years in *The Gypsies*.

The Second World War and the persecution of the Gypsies under the Nazis ended the idyllic years. By force of circumstances the Gypsies and I became involved in underground activities. In early 1943 a large group of us was arrested by the *Geheime Feld Polizei*. Interrogated under duress, we were eventually condemned to death. After six months captivity I was miraculously saved by being released through an administrative error. I resumed resistance operations organizing escape routes between Germany and Spain. When the route was detected by the Germans I escaped into Spain after a harrowing crossing of the Pyrenees. I was interned in the Spanish concentration camp of Miranda del Ebro. After my release, and awaiting my transfer to England and further service, I lived with the Gypsies in Spain. My second book *Crossing* deals with this period.

Jan Yoors

Introduction

In Spain, as nowhere else, oppression has wrought a change in the Gypsy character. It is in Flamenco singing, dancing and guitar playing that the Gypsies find an outlet for their rebellious instincts and express their singularity.

CONTRARY to my original, and certainly more romantic, intentions, and against all expectation, this book grew to be a shout of frantic wonderment, a shout of anguish and passion, in the tradition perhaps of the *cante grande*, "alternating between throaty cries of pain and soaring evocations of ecstasy" for those Spain branded "the most despised and haughty of races." In this sense, *The Gypsies of Spain* is in sharp contrast to an earlier book I wrote about the first six idyllic years I spent among the *Rom*, the nomadic Gypsies who wander through Europe. As I wrote then, I intended that to be "a protest against oblivion, a cry of love for this race of strangers who have lived among us for centuries and remained apart."

The *Rom* travel extensively, covering entire continents. Since the Second World War, I have lived with them, a few months at a time, in places as far afield as Uzbekistan in the southeastern U.S.S.R., and Peru and Brazil at the other geographic extreme, with many places in between. Even though they travel in relatively small bands, *kumpania*, they possess a significant sense of being part of a larger whole. These Gypsies remain by their own definition "hunters," with hunter's privileges. They travel in part to avoid inbreeding and to meet as yet unknown relatives, as much as to avoid depletion of their "grazing territories," that is, they move on before the tolerance of the host country wears out and persecution threatens. Their migration forms part of a continuing, worldwide cultural transfusion and an ever-flowing force of renewal.

Over the centuries, since the time they came out of India, the *Rom* have remained fluid in their apparent adaptation to changing terrain and people; yet, in their own way, they have been as consistent as water and as incorruptible, with the fierce will to be separate and to survive.

Again the survival and circumstances of the *Gitanos* are in total contrast to that of the *Rom*.

Some years ago, while traveling through the Negev Desert, I read a description that has haunted me ever since as relevant to the phenomenon of the *Gitanos*: "the Dead Sea is really a vast lake, into which the waters of the Jordan River flow and are lost by evaporation. But the natural salts remain, making the sea extremely bitter to the tongue and giving it a wonderful buoyancy."

It is, of course, a fact that most countries through which the Gypsies pass on their endless migration have attempted to assimilate them under extreme duress and terror "for all the right reasons" and "to improve their lot." The reappearance or survival of the nomadic *Rom* proves how unsuccessful the attempts at repression, assimilation, or genocide have been.

Yet in Spain, save for brief intermissions, the tradition of persecution has continued persistently. And there, as nowhere else, has oppression wrought as deep a change in the Gypsy character. Cut off from most avenues of escape, many were driven into special Gypsy quarters and, with varying degrees of success, were Hispanized. Small groups escaped into the wild, mountainous regions of southern Spain. They "submerged" to blossom out at intervals into such exotic flower as the art of Flamenco by which this race expressed its singularity.

Even those who were assimilated into Spanish Catholic culture remained at best baptized heathen suspected of retaining a consciousness different from the dominant norm. From true Gypsies, they became disinherited. In many cases it appears nothing survived beyond the recollection of Gypsy descent; yet they were made to suffer for the ways of their forefathers of which they themselves were ignorant. Today the vast majority of them has lost the understanding and the speaking knowledge of *Calo*, which in its known form, as recorded by George Borrow in 1841 in the translation of the New Testament, was already then heavily Hispanized. They were ostracized to prevent the "pollution of the race." The Spaniards were anxious to maintain *limpieza de sangre*, that mythical purity of blood untainted by Moorish, Jewish, or Gypsy blood, even though the Moors had married into Spain for seven hundred years and the Jews for possibly much longer.

After centuries of relentless and terrible persecution, it is a wonder that the *Gitanos* have survived at all. And still the past persists, the old ways linger on. The *Gitanos* have retained above all an amazing resilience, uncontrollable, exploding with tempestuous abandon, in bursts of reckless unconcern. It is in Flamenco singing, dancing, and guitar playing they find an outlet for their rebellious instincts, which they voice with an almost unparalleled intensity, at times too strident, too insistent for Western ears.

The *Gitanos* were driven into *Gitanerias* or Gypsy ghettoes, just as there were *Morerias*, ghettoes for Moors, and of course *Juderias* for Jews. Recently, while discussing

the subject with a Spanish acquaintance, he added what he no doubt considered a good joke: *"y monos en Monerias,"* and monkeys in monkey houses. Somewhat redundantly he added, "after all, dignity springs from order and order admits no strays."

The nomadic *Rom* know neither time nor frontiers. They should be seen detached from the host country through which they pass, like the shadows of clouds wandering against an endless sky projected on the land.

To understand and appreciate the *Gitanos,* an explanation of Spain is essential. If the *Rom* are "forever wild," the *Gitanos* are, by contrast, the "trapped ones."

As far as the world at large was concerned, the Gypsies of Spain were forgotten for centuries, until discovered, or rediscovered, along with the romanticized Andalusia of the Moorish past, by the prophets of the French romantic movement. Prosper Mérimée and Bizet created *Carmen*; Théophile Gautier wrote his *Voyage en Espagne*; Victor Hugo gave us *Esmeralda*; Richepin wrote the popular novel *Miarka la fille á l'ours*; Gustave Doré did illustrations of the *Gitanos* of the Monte Sagrado; Baudelaire wrote his poem *La tribu prophétique aux prunelles ardentes*. There were also Alexander Dumas and Washington Irving. And last but not least there was George Borrow, the most inspired and unlikely British Gypsy-lover-evangelist-adventurer-writer who published his *Zincali,* the Bible in Spanish, *Romany Ray*, and *Lavengro* to popular acclaim.

In Spain itself, there was the Golden Age of Flamenco which culminated in the *café cantante* of the nineteenth century. In the first quarter of the twentieth, under the inspiring drive of *aficionados* like Manuel de Falla, Federico García Lorca, the painter Ignacio Zuologa and others, the first Flamenco contest was held in the rehabilitated Generaliffe Gardens and the Alhambra of Granada in 1922.

In our time, through the medium of tourist pamphlets and travel agency posters, Flamenco and the *Gitanos* have once again, much to the impatience of the Spaniards themselves, become as emblematic of Spain as the *Folies Bergères* used to be of France, or the Blues or Dixieland Jazz might be of the United States.

Guidebooks alluringly describe Gypsy Quarters. Upon inquiry, though, I found very little information available and all of it quite inaccurate to boot. Whatever had been promised was never delivered. On the whole the Spanish, proud of their own heritage, tended to belittle into nothing the contributions of the *Gitanos*. Whenever I persisted in finding out more about them, where and how they lived, it was patronizingly suggested I catch the show at 11 P.M. at the Tablao where commerical Flamenco music and dancing was presented. I encountered mostly indifference if not outright coldness and reproach. Once the subject was simply and brusquely dismissed as just a lurid anomaly, to the extent it made me wonder about the envy that lurks behind such moral condemnation.

"The *Gitanillos* [like they would have said the Darkies] live in the south. They sing, they dance, even when they have nothing in their little bellies!" "They all live in Triana, across the Guadalquivir from Sevilla." I was told that was the true Soulsville. "No, not any longer. Now they all live in the Sacromonte section of Granada." When there I was told, "No they all went away." "They are all good Catholics now and are assimilated."

It was somehow difficult at first to dismiss the acquired illusion until I was at last forced to look for myself, without much assistance, but with fresh eyes unimpeded by what others have seen. What I found was a startlingly inverted image, like the one seen in a concave mirror.

Chapter 1
Feria

The exuberant Feria of Sevilla, the tone of which is essentially Flamenco, as a climactic introduction to Andalucia.

IT was late at night. The air was warm and languid with the overwhelming fragrance of orange blossoms and jasmine. I was once again in Sevilla and a shiver of delight went through me. I surrendered to the experience.

Yesterday I had still been across the ocean, in New York, doing the last hectic mandatory things "that couldn't wait" until I had to wrench myself loose, with a tinge of regret for all that remained unfinished.

I walked leisurely and without clear purpose through the warrenlike passageways of the Barrio de Santa Cruz, narrow like slits. Everywhere I heard the rustle of people moving through the night and the sound of nailstudded shoes rebounding off the silent houses. A thread of wood smoke mingled with the smell of olive oil. Overhead I heard the harsh, hurried, unharmonious bell of the *Giralda*. It lasted only very briefly and was like a joyful clashing of coal shovels. The *Giralda*, that symbol and pride of Sevilla, is a great square minaret which was later incorporated in the Christian cathedral built after the reconquest of Spain from the Moors. It was lit by powerful floodlights and over it, detached in the light against the night sky, large unidentifiable birds circled and wavered eerily.

Very near the cathedral stands the Barrio de Santa Cruz, the quaint old Jewish ghetto, which for me is one of the most romantic places on earth.

A strange, rhythmic cadence of many hands clapping in unison rose out of the darkened passageways. A wordless song that would end abruptly. Like the drumming of rain stops suddenly to be replaced by a silence even deeper than before. Then from another direction, but distinctly moving toward me, the rhythmic clapping started again. It was rapid and even, slightly muffled. Then that, too, stopped suddenly. The beat was accompanied by no other sound. It was a thing in itself, with its own reason, its own logic. There were no crescendoes. They did not, as far as I could make out, answer each other or take clues from the others. Each group seemed to function independently. It fascinated me, but its meaning was lost to me. The duration of the clapping varied as did the interruptions. Its abrupt end was as crisp as its beginning. The unison was perfect. Walking along the street, I passed a group of men, women, young and old. Mysteriously, the clapping started within my hearing and observation. No command was given. The regularity of the cadence bore no constraining or military qualities. I could not decide for myself if it was joyous or solemn. It had perhaps something of cicadas. . . .

Sevilla—the warm, humming night, the distinctly alternating or overlapping rustle, and the abrupt cessation of all sound were haunting.

After I stopped for a glass of wine and a plate of prawns, I resumed my leisurely wandering. I inhaled deeply the enchanted night. The twisting, winding narrow passages were bordered by unbroken, trimly whitewashed garden walls over the tops of which vines casually overflowed. Through open doors, closed off by wrought iron grills, I caught glimpses of well lit, inviting patios with pots of geraniums, carnations, sweet basil, and asparagus plants, massed together on the flagstone or sienna-colored tile floors. Small fountains trickled discreetly or murmured seductively. Everywhere I looked, there was an overabundance of unabashed charm. Most of the cobblestone streets were so narrow that they allowed only pedestrians through. Overhead, the balconies seemed about to reach the houses on the opposite side of the passageway. Street level windows had intricate wrought iron grills, bristling with spikes, bulging out into the street like the profile of a handwritten letter "d" in lower case. Unwilling to break the spell, I walked aimlessly for hours, winding into stretches I had wandered through before, becoming gradually more familiar with specific features, making friends, as it were. The mysterious clapping of hands went on unabated. The overall hum was occasionally embroidered upon by the hollow sound of horsehoofs trotting.

Unexpectedly, I emerged from the now familiar environment of closed houses, pale as chalk or ghost, permeated beyond description by the heady hothouse fragrance of orange blossoms. In front of me opened up a narrow stretch of astoundingly luminous yellow soil with tall palm trees swaying slightly. Violets and roses grew at the foot of the trees. A large festive crowd was milling about. The women and little girls wore long dresses with ruffles, flowers and high combs in their hair. The men wore stiff, wide-brimmed felt hats, grey or black, with a flattened crown, white shirts and ties, with tight-fitting short jackets. There were many riders on magnificent mounts parading and wheeling about.

In the distance I saw a fantastic construction blazing with thousands of electric light bulbs. Along the Calle San Fernando, by the old tobacco factory, stood a huge ornamental gate flanked by the facade of a building à la Potemkin. It was built only for the duration of the *Feria* (Fair) and served as a grandiose gateway, worthy of an Arabian sultan, to the fairground proper.

I was faced by a burst of colors and light, and assailed by a cacophony for which the introspective penumbra of the narrow, private alleyways of the Barrio de Santa Cruz —where the only sound was of receding or approaching waves of clapping hands, the occasional hollow sound of horsehooves, or the discreet tinkle of fountains—had not prepared me. Along the boulevards was row upon row of temporary pavillions with wooden partitions and brightly striped canvas roofs, called *casetas*. They were extravagantly decorated and belonged to the best families of Andalusia—although a few be-longed to religious brotherhoods, private clubs, and a few forward looking commercial firms—in which they proudly received and lavishly entertained their friends, relatives, or clients. There was an abundance of food and drink, music, dancing, and laughter.

Everything was Flamenco, or *Gitano,* from the best of the gay music, in this case the *Sevillanas,* the extravaganza of polka dot dresses in bright yellows and mauves, blues, and flaming reds and pinks; and the dances were voluptuous, "Gypsy-like." The guests participated by lustily clapping hands in encouragement and accompaniment. Hundreds of magnificent horsemen paraded up and down without end. The air was impregnated by the smell of horses, charcoal fires, and seafood. There was a constant throbbing hum of snorting or neighing horses, the grinding of wheels of the numerous horse-drawn carriages, the distant drone of guitars, the clinking of glasses and the clatter of dishes, the clicking of heels and the perennial clapping of hands. It was like fireworks against the velvet black sky. The festivities reached fever pitch yet, strangely enough, without the revelers for a single instant losing their courteous formality or their almost Victorian sense of propriety.

I felt drunk with all the magic of the smells, tastes, sights, colors, and sounds of Sevilla. I felt happy and carefree. Time was blotted out.

This night was a splendid reintroduction to Spain, and I fully realized it had started with a climax. I knew few other fairs the world over could match it. I was carried along in a kind of megalomaniac euphoria reluctant to break the spell, reluctant to admit to myself it was only a hallucination. I was in a world which had nothing in common with yesterday; almost like a visit to the vanished Russia of Gogol or Chekhov.

As twilight approached, I tore myself away from the scene—I could not really admit to its reality—picturesque to a fault.

Horsemen still paraded and rode around, and the general revelry went on unabated, with panache, full of grace and wit, gay, flamboyant, romantic.

It was the epitome of *Andalucismo,* the

spirit of the southern provinces, that love of life and exuberance which those of Castilla and Christian Spain—as exemplified by *Casticismo*—brands as *Gitano* or Moorish. They said this with rancor, and emphatically. The *Feria* of Sevilla reflected *Andalucismo* at its most passionate culmination in this annual explosion. *Casticismo* represented the raw austerity of the Castillian highlands attempting since centuries past to impose centralism on plural Spain. It was the somber grandeur of Spain at once tragic and defiant. It was the mad integrity, the brooding over the disintegration of flesh—as if denying the immortality claimed by Catholicism—and the suicidal concept of honor and dignity. It was the unresolved polarity between Christian north and the sediment of Islam of the south, born from, and intensified through, the centuries of the Reconquest.

I walked home slowly through enchanted Sevilla humming to myself melodies of the gay *Sevillanas.* The narrow streets were quiet and a new day dawned.

I woke up late to the unaccustomed clatter of horsehooves coming and going in every direction. I had difficulty at first recovering a sense of time and place, but I also had difficulty recovering a sense of my own identity. It was with an unaccustomed sense of morning-after guilt that I telephoned home, as I had promised I would, and the long distance call to New York became my only link to reality.

I had a late Spanish breakfast with *café con leche,* one-quarter strong coffee with three-quarters milk served in tall, narrow glasses, and rich golden-brown *churros,* deep fried, narrow strips of dough, eggs fried in olive oil with tomatoes, peppers, and onions, garnished with a few tips of asparagus and green peas. There were only men. The ladies were still resting from the previous night's exertion, or had breakfast in their own apartments. The atmosphere was comradely and open. They all knew one another. From the conversation I learned they were mostly landowners of large estates, *latifundios,* or of *ganaderos,* ranches breeding bulls for the bullfights, from all over Andalusia. They met here in Sevilla during the week for the *Feria*

and this residence near the Plaza de los Reyes was their exclusive gathering spot. Most of them were middle-aged or over, well-groomed, without in any way losing their healthy outdoor ruddiness. They radiated charm and earthiness, dignity and bonhomie. They were dressed in formal, dark riding clothes, and white shirts with lace or embroidery at the front and throat. Several of them already had strapped on their handsome, hand-tooled riding chaps and spurs.

At the door in the blazing sunlight waited the stable grooms with the riding horses. The Arabian steeds had long flowing tails and manes. The saddles were high and with great box stirrups. How appropriate to these gentlemen was the inscription often seen on walls all over the city, like an inspirational motto, "nothing if not a man." They spoke with the slurred pronunciation of the south and with a tendency to swallow the word-endings, offending the pure and stately vernacular of Castilla. These gentlemen represented everything which further north would be put down, with a sneer and possibly with envy, as "south of the Ebro."

After finishing a last morning brandy, the men swung into the saddle and moved at a gallop from the dignified elegance of the Hotel Doña Maria into the world of horse sweat, dust, and blazing sunshine. They left in small groups of relatives and friends, and perhaps with a discreet admission of hierarchy. If there was a touch of masculine obsession in their ways, it was tempered with manly grace, wit, a sophisticated casualness and self-assured nonchalance. From all over Sevilla horsemen rode to the *paseo,* to see and to be seen.

Later in the day, the married women and the very young followed them to the fairground, riding in a variety of carriages. According to type, these were drawn by smart teams of mules, a pair of Arabians, or better yet by four, six, and sometimes eight horses —with the added flourish of a ninth horse in the lead—with superbly cocksure coachmen to handle them with competence and style. These were often dressed in flamboyant liveries as eighteenth-century operatic smugglers, or they wore unlikely *kufiya* (Bedouin or Near Eastern Arab cotton headdress) and *aghal* (double twisted cord worn over the *kufiya* as a headband) and were disguised as *Druse* (eleventh-century religious minority, mystical offshoot of Islam, living in Syria and northern Israel). Others wore high hats. But they all drove in fierce competition, intent at all cost to do their masters proud.

Those who rode in the carriages, in sharp contrast, seemed relaxed and benevolent as if unaware of the competition between the teams, or mildly amused by it and utterly unconcerned with possible damage or danger to others.

Mingling with the stream of coaches weaving in and out was a young couple. The man proudly in the saddle, the girl in all her finery mounted side-saddled behind him, with her right arm wound around his waist, the other hand, in a fist, set provocatively at her waist.

The horses pranced, frisked, reared, and milled around, snorting and neighing, as two unending columns paraded past each other in opposite direction.

A heavyset rider yielded momentarily to a desire to pose, made his horse rear, and kept him in that impossible position, like they did so well in the old Western movies. In fact, much reminded me of the old Western movies, except that both the set and the cast were at least fifty times larger than the make-believe one. It was happening for real, here, now, and with shameless delight, I was part of it.

Proudly riding beside their fathers were three- and four-year-old boys, and on a few occasions little girls, simulating to perfection their elders' arrogance. I secretly hoped, for their sake, that they were properly strapped to the saddle.

A robust rider with short, iron-grey hair slowed down his horse, one of the handsomest I had seen of possibly five or six hundred. The man was noticeably unsmiling and withdrawn. He proceeded to give us a rare display of horsemanship, that of a horseman's horseman. Mount and rider created an unmoving obstacle in the flow of horses until these split up without changing pattern or slackening their pace, to allow a fairly large open space for the demonstration. The rider put his horse through an in-

tricate dance step pattern. Holding up high and rigid the right front leg, the horse moved in circles in a mincing step on three legs, alternating a few steps by holding up the left front leg. He hobbled forward holding the two front legs and the two hind ones together. Sitting low on his haunches, he pawed the air with his front legs like a dog begging for food. He moved in extra slow movements with quivering hindquarters. He moved in quickstep, making narrower and narrower figure eight's and moved his head up and down, punctuating the unaccustomed jerky movements with a flourish, as if to acknowledge the attention his master and he were getting—and asking for. The rider gave low voice commands and hardly seemed to prod or guide his horse in any other visible way.

There was a steady movement of horse carriages, victorias, landaus, and barouches, as they vied for the right-of-way. High-spirited horses became restive. There also were carriages for hire at exorbitant rates, driven by jolly drivers, for city dwellers of lesser means. At the time of the *Feria* the Sevillans of any standing, even more so than usual, lived and behaved extravagantly in a display of gaiety and improvident generosity, to a fault.

The incomparable parade of horses, fashion, and handsome citizens went on for hours under a burning sun. The horsemen drank in the saddle and ate without dismounting. Groups met in front of specific *casetas* and were offered stirrup-cups, mostly of the very pale, slightly sour, dry white wine from around Sanlucar, from Chiclana de la Frontera, or from the estate of the particular family who entertained. Sometimes brandy or anise was offered. The owner of each *caseta* tried to outdo all others in the quality of food he offered, the elegance of serving it, not to mention the lavish profusion of it—in truly regal indulgence.

For those not invited, or welcome, to the private *casetas* of the great families, the clubs, or the syndicates, there were at the far end of the fairground, along Avenida de Portugal, long rows of stalls catering to the hoi poloi, who so as not to be outdone on this occasion celebrated with the lusty flamboyance of another age.

24

Wooden tables, benches, and low stools had been set out onto the paved street and partly onto the yellow earth sidewalk where large family groups enjoyed the shared food. At each stall different specialties were prepared and sold: hard roll sandwiches, *bocadillos*, with *jamon serrano*, the sweet-salt, crunchy ham cured in the Sierra Morena; cold omelets, grilled veal; seafood—mullet and sole lightly dipped in flour and fried in olive oil, small orange crabs, bright pink boiled shrimps, and baby squids. There was also an abundance of almond and sesame seed pastries, anise cakes, and deep fried fritters "made of wind," *de viento*. For the Sevillans had inherited from their Moorish past an almost Oriental liking for sweets.

During the hot hours of the day, people ate only light snacks. After the *siesta* at five in the afternoon, so succinctly sung in Federico García Lorca's elegy for Ignacio Sanchez Mejias, people went to the bull-fight at the magnificent Maestranza Arena by the Guadalquivir River. Posters announcing the *corridas* were all over Sevilla. This anachronistic spectacle, emphatically declared art and not sport, formed an integral part of Spanish life. Unlike in many other places, and against the demands and innovations of modernism, this ritualistic drama, evocative of archaic Altamira, Lascaux, and Minoa, was preserved in Sevilla in its most classical manner.

In the late afternoon, once again horsemen and carriages converged on the fairground to begin the revelry that would last until dawn.

It was unusually hot for April, even for Sevilla. For several days the *Feria* had been going at full tilt, with little time wasted on sleep. The general mood was easy-going and exuberant, frothy, with endless singing, handclapping, and group dancing in which everybody participated. All young people and children were dressed in Flamenco—bright colors of undulating ripples of full-scallopped skirts and bodices tightly molding the torsos. They wore high combs and flowers in the hair and big, spectacular earrings. Flamenco, that evocative, alluring, but indefinable concept, was generally accepted to mean Gypsy. The dancing was Flamenco. The music was Flamenco. The very style of life was Flamenco. The Andalusians gathered here in Sevilla from all over the provinces, camping out in temporary *casetas*, eating, drinking, and dancing—were they not like storybook *Gitanos*?

I heard a certain Don Miguel, a man of consequence, authority, and wealth, buoyant with an obvious joy for life, described admiringly as *que tio más Gitano* "very much of a Gypsy." When I asked about his being a *Gitano*, he answered with a sarcastic, incredulous counter question: *"Gitano Gitano? Claro que no!"* "Gypsy Gypsy? Certainly not!"

I realized that the adjective *Gitano* was not meant radically or literally but more to denote rascal, said in fun or in admiration; somebody full of life, irrepressible, somebody with wit and charm, frivolous and vain, mischievous perhaps. But *Gitano, Gitano, claro que no*. Never. Inconceivable. My question had been brusquely dismissed, yet the gay little song I heard immediately after dealt again, obsessively it seemed, with a *Gitanilla*, a little Gypsy girl.

I became aware that I had not seen any *Gitanos* at the *Feria* for all these days. In the early morning hours while walking home, I heard *Cante Hondo* sung unmistakably by a true Flamenco perfomer in one of the *casetas*; I meant sung by a true Gypsy, but Flamenco and *Gitano* overlapped, blended, and were hard to tell apart, and in this respect the Sevillans were of no help.

Dance, music, abundant food, pale dry sherry, sultry heat, colorful crowds, horsemen, carriages, the fragrance of orange blossoms, mixed with smells of charcoal, the roasting of lean meats, and horse sweat dazed me pleasantly, made me forget and led me to postpone my inquiry.

Nights and days ran into each other until they were indistinguishable. Like the *Sevillanas* themselves, those gay rhythms, beyond a point, became monotonously gay, senselessly gay, ephemerally gay, without building up in intensity, without ever reaching a climax.

Suddenly I felt overwhelmed by an almost physical incompatibility. Seeking relief and to renew contact with another side of Spain, and to counteract the frivolity, I decided to visit the cathedral.

Chapter 2
Love of Life

Haunting, unresolved polarity between Christian Spanish preoccupation with death and dying and the Islamic sediment of Andalusian love of life and sensual enjoyment.

FROM the sultry heat I entered a cold twilight. There was a sudden stillness and a solemn mystery. The air was heavy with stale incense. The senses were overwhelmed as violently as they had been by the harsh sunlight and the activities of the *Feria* itself. At first all I sensed was the majestic size of the muffled echoing cavern. As my eyesight adjusted to the shadows, I noticed through the twilight a blaze of candlelight at the far side of the cathedral. I saw, jumbled at first, huge golden grilles, opulent silver altars, and the exuberant prodigy of Spanish Baroque of unimaginable splendor: polychrome statues of saints, Flemish altar screens.

This was the largest Gothic building in the world. It had over eighty private chapels, in some of which more than fifty masses were celebrated daily. In the distance I heard rumbling organ music. Very loud and very solemn and very Spanish. The interior of the building was blackened by centuries of smoky candlelight. Against this background, the superfluity, the confusion of much gold, had a cumulative spellbinding effect. It built up a somber, tragic power to the Glory of God and the consolation of the poor in their poverty.

Mitres of dead bishops were suspended from the high vaults over the marble gravestone of each. A popular belief had it that the mitres disintegrated whenever the church officials who had worn them ascended to Heaven, having in Purgatory expiated their sins. "Judge for yourself," I was told, "how many cardinals and bishops are still there and how numerous must have been their sins."

In front of me rose, tremendous in size, the catafalque of Christopher Columbus, carried aloft by four giant-size Baroque figures. That obstinate visionary Cristobál Colón, whom we chose to call Christopher Columbus, was of disputed national origin. Genoa claims him, and so does Barcelona. The Spanish historian Salvador de Madariaga, in a study of his personal letters, sought to prove him to be a Galician Jew.

There are also many theories about the grave of Columbus. The Sevilla one, though forever unverified, states that upon his death in Valladolid, bitterly disillusioned, having known struggle, triumph, and disgrace, he was buried in Santo Domingo. At a later date, and for reasons unsatisfactorily explained, his remains were removed to Havana, Cuba; and it was only after Spain lost her last colonies in the New World he had discovered that, at last, his bones found their final resting place in Sevilla.

A shaft of sunlight slashed the dim atmosphere, revealing more harshly the barbaric splendor, and in the crude light of day much of the mystery was lessened.

Several very young choirboys in ornate surplices hurried across the nave. A canon read his missal in the dimly lit *coro*. In Spanish churches, the *coro,* or choir, is placed in the middle of the nave, a church within a church, breaking up the long diagonal vistas.

I sat down and let myself daydream, adrift through confused memories. I felt as if I were back in some familiar past, back in a world I had known as a child.

Images, exotically mysterious, and haunting recollections, conceivably surpressed, of Holy Week surged forth.

The night was dark and quiet. It was the

hour before daybreak. Through the narrow streets, far from the center, a slow procession moved closer, like ghosts of Medieval Spain. A funeral procession of hooded figures, with slits for the eyes, carrying at an angle from the hip, long, lighted, flickering tapers. They were barefoot and dragged six-feet-long lengths of chains which rattled over the cobbled stones. Several black satin ghostlike figures in tall conical hoods staggered forward, dragging massive wooden crosses, large enough for them to be crucified upon. A drum beat a muffled funeral half step, dreadful and sad like an execution.

In a flash of heightened, or hallucinatory, perception I could not dissociate from these images of magical potency the sinister heritage of the *Auto de Fé*, Acts of Faith, culminating with burnings at the stake, of the *Suprema*, the Holy Office of the Inquisition. The voluntary penitents, proud members of today's *Cofradías,* shuffling by before me were living survival of the old flagellation sects. I felt awed by the pageantry and equally stunned by the grim reality implied in the apperance.

Between the barefoot, hooded penitents in chains walked agents of the *Guardia Civil,* wrapped against the night chill in their long greatcoats. And they wore shiny black tricornered hats. One of them had a moustache as narrow as an eyebrow. They looked aloof, arrogant, powerful, and indifferent. I shuddered with a forgotten fright.

The excess of the Inquisition had somehow, for the world at large, become synonymous with Spain. Whenever torture was used in the interrogation cell of any nameless prison, it was qualified as Inquisitorial.

The Spaniards, with pride or indifference, dismissed these charges simply as detailed falsehood, part of the *Leyenda Negra,* the Black Legend about an obscurantist, cruel, and fanatical Spain raised against them by some unaccountable streak of malice and treachery of their political enemies, the Dutch and English heretics, protestants to others, and the *Maranos,* the Sephardic Jews exiled from Spain.

The literature about the Inquisition circulating in Spain today presents the tribunal as an essential and saving component of the nation's structure created in the Golden Age by the legendary Catholic Monarchs. For three-and-a-half centuries thereafter, it was to represent all that was sacred in the heritage of a religious people. The Spaniards righteously maintain that any derogatory evidence is slanted by partisan interpretation.

The horrors of the Inquisition, it is sadly true, were not uniquely Spanish. As with so many things, though, they were being carried to belated extremes in Spain when they were already waning in Western Europe.

In this context it may be relevant to remember that as late as 1761, in the century of enlightenment and the Encyclopedist, Jews in Nancy, France, were burned after having been mercifully strangulated; and at the Old Bailey, in London in 1786, a woman was executed and burned for the crime of false coining."

In historic fact, the Inquisition was initiated by Pope Innocent III as part of the crusade against the Albigensian and the Waldensian heretics in Languedoc and Provence, in southern France, in anticipation of Protestantism. It was also he who introduced the infamous yellow Jewish badge.

The procedure of the Inquisition was characterized by the secrecy of the trial based on anonymous denunciations and the use of torture to extort confessions. The sentences ranged all the way from public penance to life imprisonment. Stubborn heretics who refused to recant, or those who relapsed into heresy, were turned over to the secular government to be burned at the stake. *Quemado vivo,* burned alive, was sometimes also described as "without effusion of blood," a euphemism based on the quotation of John the Evangelist (15.6) "if a man abide not in me, he is cast forth as a branch and is withered; and men gather them and cast them into the fire and they are burned. . . ." In 1233, Pope Gregory IX established the Permanent Commission.

At that particular time, Spain resolutely opposed the establishment of the Holy Office of the Inquisition. It was only in the fifteenth century that the Holy Office acquired plenary authority and fully embarked, for the following three centuries, upon its career of blood in the kingdom and its dependencies. Ostensibly the aim was to clear the realm of heresy.

Until the forcible mass conversion of Jews and Moslems, there had been in Spain a considerable body of nonbelievers outside the Catholic church. These were easily singled out and controlled by a series of clerical and governmental regulations. After 1391, however, there were the same number of *conversos* inside the fold. Forced baptism had done little more than convert a large number of Jews and Moslems from infidels outside the church to heretics inside it.

Sinister, capricious, and unappealable, the Inquisition condemned not only deed but thought. It unleashed a terrible passion for hurting. All trust was lost, and suspicion bred menace as the declared friend might well be a secret foe. It encouraged jealousy and greed. All property of those condemned was seized by the tribunal. Arbitrary confiscations became an incitement for callous rapacity. It enforced rigid conformity at the price of suffocating intellectual initiative and scientific research. Out of its righteousness, the tribunal stated what God willed, as oppression evolved a logic of its own. The Inquisition's misguided zeal, exaggerated sense of loyalty, and relentlessness were worthy of a better cause. In order to save Spain and Christianity, they created forms presumed necessary and rituals that obscured the teaching of Christ and the message of love.

One time when I wandered through the grass-covered, gently rolling hills, sparsely dotted with oak trees and abundant purple thistles of Upper Galilee, I had wondered and in silence, and with unwept tears, greeted the pathetic hordes of forgotten victims, tormented and destroyed in His name.

In the grandiose pastoral peacefulness it dawned on me that the Spanish church had ceased to be universal, for such sins bear their own punishment; the victors suffered as terribly as the vanquished, though differently. Centuries of slow stagnation set in and Spain began to waste away. I had been aware, as you were aware, through hearsay of this schizophrenic neverland, of that eternity of terror, only as one peers over the protective edge of a well to guardedly probe but never fully appreciate its depth.

Toward the end of the Second World War, as an Allied liaison agent with the Maquis, I was arrested by the Nazis and was exposed to secular Inquisitorial treatment.

In the coming twilight I watched a while longer as the hooded penitents shuffled by, followed by the enormous float, or *paso,* with an eerie, life-size Christ figure nailed on the cross, depicted with grim realism as perhaps, with the exception of the German painter Grünewald, only the Spanish were capable of. Coagulated blood, sweat, tears, and gore in emphatic clinical details. At each corner of the *paso* stood Roman soldiers in military regalia. The float was carried on the shoulders and heads of men, paid men, who were hidden from view by a curtain covering the lower part of the construction. It swayed gently as it moved forward and occasionally lurched or pitched. The vast cloudless sky became opalescent in the oncoming twilight. They marched like this from before sunup of the first day to Friday of Holy Week; they march from every parish of Sevilla, twenty or more of them every day to a grand total of about one hundred and fifty, to gather at the Cathedral.

Next to the *pasos* commemorating in the form of a tableau the Passion and the Death of Christ, there were four score dedicated to the Virgin, Mother of God. Somewhat unaccountably, they were considered the central figures of the procession. There was the *Virgen de la Esperanza,* of Hope, from across the river, much beloved by the people, and her float was by far the most ornate. There was the prodigious *Virgen de la Macarena,* young and glamorous, improbably named after a Moorish Princess. There was Our Lady of Tears, the Virgin of Victory, and the Fifth Anguish of the Most Holy Mary. None of the Virgins of Sevilla carried a child and in age they seemed the same age as the Christ figure itself. There was a statue of Our Lord of the Good Death and of *Jesu*

Cristo of the Great Power. The statues of the Virgin on some *pasos* were weighted down with elaborate jewelry of inestimable value; others had silken canopies supported by twisted columns of massive silver.

The floats were preceded by heralds who, bearing heavy wooden staves with iron rings, pounded the pavement with a harsh jangling rhythm. Others were accompanied by the solemn blare of bugles playing martial music. There were bishops and flocks of penitents and heavily armed units of *Guardia Civil*, marching companies of soldiers with loaded guns, and politicians and officeholders.

At close range, the smell of incense and sweat and cut flowers momentarily overpowered that of orange blossoms and jasmine.

The various processions came to Sierpes, that narrow pedestrian thoroughfare that to its citizens was the essence of Sevilla. The large, unwieldy floats inched their way through. This was the high point of the parade.

In doorways or balconies, at every possible point of vantage and behind the big plate glass window of the cassino, there was a dense, noisy, cheerful crowd, dressed in their Sunday best and in a holiday mood.

The juxtaposed images were completely surreal—an emaciated Christ figure on the cross, bleeding from nails driven through hands and feet, slowly gliding past a pastry shop, and the double line of penitents filing past garish displays of postcards.

The bands loudly played the somber music of Passion Week. Unexpectedly, a shrill, animal scream rang out, weird and loud and as out of place as would have been the call to prayer of the *muezzin*. It was followed by a hushed stillness as the otherwise somewhat irreverent crowd paid the homage of silence. It was the beginning of a *saeta,* or what in Spanish was described as an arrow song, a cry in violent praise to God or the Virgin, with words about His suffering, or Her grief as His Mother. It was powerful and moving, raucous and intense, deep, wild, and almost inhuman. The hypnotic *saetas,* like Negro spirituals, were secularized hymns.

The disembodied voice rose and fell, drowning out all else, dominating the scene. The singer was a Gypsy and he sang as in a trance, at first as if groping his way before the soaring flight. It gripped one at the soul and clutched at the throat. There was a startlingly long pause; as if overwhelmed by emotion, he choked on the sound too powerful and beyond his control that was to surge out of him. It was what Federico García Lorca meant when he said "they make their voices sound like gushing blood." There was no other sound and the tension was unbearable. Then the weird cry resumed with visceral intensity modulated, rising, rising, deliriously, like a lark in the endless sky, immediate and remote. It had a strange bruised quality which was distinctly not of the Western Christian world. The crowds responded by listening with an intensity equal to his.

The words of the *saetas* were improvised, spontaneous, and colloquial. The mighty lament ended as awkwardly as it had started, as if choked into silence, overcome by emotion unlike any other song I have ever heard.

In jarring counterpoint, *Sierpes* rang with the resonant cadence of hobnailed boots, the tapping of the iron-tipped staves, the tatoo of martial drums and undercurrent of excited murmur of the onlookers. The line of penitents moved on, followed by floats, ecclesiastical and lay dignitaries, soldiers, with pomp and majesty rolling on like a surging sea.

The Passion of the Lord was to Spain the high point of spring and Easter, as the Resurrection of Christ was to the Russian Orthodox Church. Easter in Spain meant the resuming of the bullfighting season. The bullfighting was known as the *Fiesta de la Luz,* or celebration of light. In fact, if it was not a celebration of death, then at least it was a spectacle at which death was an inevitable guest.

I emerged from my daydreaming and half-memories. The day had waned and by now the inside of the cathedral was dark, and it was chilly as a morgue. The darkness made the candlelight seem even brighter. I walked out into the purple-cast evening light and lingered at the Patio de los Naranjos, the court of the orange trees, that serene enclosed Moorish garden with row upon row of trees in full bloom. It was unpretentious and an unexpected haven of peace. It reflected harmony and repose, free of the anguish over mortality everywhere else apparent.

Above me, against the darkening skies, dominating Sevilla, rose the Moorish *Giralda* tower.

Old-fashioned carriages with arms emblazoned across their sides, pulled by the trotting horses, circled the Plaza de los Reyes. Proud, handsome horsemen rode by ... I was greeted by the sound of wildly gay *Sevillanas* sung by small groups of vivacious young people strolling to the fairground.

I chose to avoid the more crowded thoroughfares like the Avenida Queipo de Llano —named after, depending on the particular political perspective, the Savior of Sevilla or the Butcher of Andalusia. I took the shortcut through my beloved Barrio de Santa Cruz, where songbirds still twittered before complete nightfall in the fruit trees of walled gardens. Again I yielded to the enchantment of the place the Moors praised as *Al Andaluz* where they could live a life of repose and sensuality, and the loss of which, symbolized by the loss of their last great city in Spain, Granada, the Moslems still today bemoan in their evening prayers.

As on every other night of the *Feria*, the spacious fairgrounds were illuminated and in full effervescence, like a tale of the Arabian Nights, yet with more a touch of Goya than of Persian miniatures.

Self-satisfied men smoked thin black cigars. They offered *piropos,* racy flatteries, to the girls passing by. Sevilla, after all, was the home of Don Juan, the prototype of which, it was said, was one Don Miguel de Mañara. One of his literary counterparts was Don Juan Tenorio, a Spanish symbol for whom romantic intrigues and amorous pursuits were closely akin to the pleasures of the hunt.

Untiringly the handsome young men on horseback paraded about with girls sitting sidesaddle in long, colorful, scallopped dresses that cascaded down over the mount's rump. The visual impression of the *Feria* was a profusion of sheer fantasy. It stirred the emotions and put the mind into a state of confused exaltation. For those few days the city was taken over by invading horsemen as if we were back in another era of old and honored values and good manners, of grace and leisure; it was a time when boisterous frivolity was but a way of getting through the day. The women looked fresh and untroubled by doubts, full-breasted, with eloquent, flirtatious eyes, fine carriages, and flowers in their hair; living was gracious and unstinting and totally free of social concern, recklessly free of any social awareness. The men's only preoccupations were, with exquisite cynicism, women, bulls, cards, and endless gossip.

I had reached a point of saturation and decided to leave the festivities. I walked back toward the Guadalquivir and the now deserted riverside. Along the way I passed Spaniards of the working class drifting from café to café celebrating the holiday. The monotonous drone of a distant guitar rose in pitch and, as I came nearer, the sounds became richer and more alluring. A blind lottery seller groped his way along the walls.

The river flowed quietly. The reflections of the lights from Triana danced on the dark water. On one side loomed the solitary Torre del Oro, the tower of gold. It reminded me that once, before Sevilla had sunken into provincial torpor and impotence, she had been the military, civil, and religious capital of the Americas. Sevilla had been the privileged Royal Port with the monopoly of the trade with the New World, held briefly before the center of commerce was transferred from Southern to Northern Europe. Here in Sevilla were stored away the archives of the Indies, the records of the *Consejo Suprema de las Indias*.

The search for *El Dorado* fired the *Conquistadores,* like Hernando Cortes, Francisco Pizarro, Nuñez de Balboa and others, to outrageously audacious military campaigns. In the next century and a half, over two hundred tons of gold entered Spain through the port of Sevilla. . . .

A Gypsy encampment is
a world entire and
distinct. The trespasser
is greeted by scrambling,
pawing, begging,
deceiving children who
protect the camp, protect
the almost invisible
vestiges of a pariah's
life. It is a life that
neither tarries nor alters,
that will leave little
evidence of its existence,
except for its ability to
persist.

The women are the energy of the life; all the chores, all that is to be done is their task.

The men tend the animals and then lean and loaf with a stance of assurance, self-sufficiency, and patience.

*Feeding on the milk of
a much suckled teat,
the young grow strong
and straight. They know
no deformity. Black
coffee, bread, and
vegetables—stealthfully
gathered—become the
standard meal.*

Heads blistering from last night's strong drink, old crones and monkey-eyed grandfathers warm their bones in the morning sun. While the women brew coffee and prepare the morning stew, the men, with clicks and hisses, call to the animals.

The Gypsies' only fear is
death and its consequent
extinction of their "way."
This fear is the demon
that drives them to swell
their families each year.
In children is the
guarantee of the Gypsies'
endurance.

Chapter 3
Horsetraders

Spanish horsetraders and Regalito; their evaluation of their own people. "There is a shadow over the Gitanos, there is a shadow over Spain."

THE following day at noon I came back to the Guadalquivir. I followed the river downstream to the yearly horsemarket at the San Sebastian meadows, which, theoretically, was the pretext for the *Feria*.

The Gypsies camped nearby on a lush, partly flooded wasteland. In the far distance some men were taking care of the horses. They moved swiftly and with a certain swagger which clearly distinguished them from the local Spaniards. The horses they possessed were superb. The encampment consisted of delapidated, open carts and badly run-down carriages in shabby disarray. Several temporary lean-to huts, held down by stones, had been improvised from the most disparate collection of tar paper, loose rotting boards, corrugated tin and bits of tarpaulins. As far as I could judge, a man could not stand upright in them. Rarely had I seen such apparent poverty or such excessive indifference to shelter and environment.

All was still. Not a dog barked, and at first I could see no activity of any kind. Slowly I crossed the wasteland when I noticed, behind a cart, two women and a very young girl crouched by a small fire preparing food.

The camp looked deserted. I realized that I could hardly expect to find anybody around while the *Feria* in Sevilla was in full swing and the horse fair on nearby. It was the middle of April but brutally hot. There was a strong smell of wild daffodils and the piercing song of the shrill cicadas.

A man lay in the shade of a lean-to. Next to him was the rattan cane, badge of the horsedealer. He watched me approach without moving. He smoked in silence; only his eyes followed me. His face had a pronounced bone structure, with regular features, large eyes under full, bushy eyebrows. His mouth was full and sensuous. The nose was aquiline and hawklike and the long, shiny hair was slightly curly. The white of eyes and teeth stood out in strong highlights. His hands were long and thin. His appearance had something feline, haughty, predatory, and enigmatic about it. I came still nearer and greeted him with a loud *"buenas tardes."* Without changing his prone position, he replied with a strange remoteness: "In what way can I be of service to you?" His nonchalant attitude suggested a restrained menace, contradicting the courteous intent of his question.

I knew the disadvantage in my making contact with him this way. I had lived many years with nomadic Gypsies and spoke their language as my own so that whenever on world-wide travels I met those I had not met before, I could use as introduction the magic Sesame of *Romani*. With the *Gitanos* I could only use Spanish, which did not distinguish me from any other *payo* or outside intruder.

He had not moved and I was standing before him awkwardly. Since he did not rise to meet me on equal ground, I squatted near him uninvited. To counter his mock quizzical look and to avoid explanations, I asked him without further ado if he knew where I could find *Hungaros*. In Spanish it meant Hungarian but was used to describe nomadic Gypsies in general. His liquid black eyes lost some of their glare. His expression changed very slightly. By appearance, I was unmistakably a *payo*. "I know the *Hungaros* well," he replied. His voice retained an edge of suspicion. "There are not many of them in this region. Whom are you looking for?" I said I had not been in Spain since 1944, when, during the world war, I had escaped the Gestapo, crossed the Pyrenees, and on arrival here had been arrested by the *Guardia Civil* and interned at the concentration camp of Miranda del Ebro. After my release, I had lived for a while with Hanzi who was married to Borinka, the daughter of Notarka, to whom my adopted *Rom* family was related. I said I would like to find any member of the families, either of Mutshoro, Notarka, Bashno or descendants of old Tshompi. I told him they had lived at the time near the Puente de Vallecas in Madrid.

He sat up as a gesture of courtesy. "Yes," he said, with a different intonation in his voice, he had heard about them. Tshompi had died a long, long time ago and he only knew about him from hearsay. Notarka also had died and several of his sons had left Spain to go to Germany and France. One had gone to South America. All those who could had left Spain. None remained here in the south. Here life was difficult. A few families of *Hungaros* were in Madrid, still near Puente de Vallecas; others were in Barcelona. "You ask when you get there. Everybody will know them."

Without getting up, he pulled from the shade of the shack a *poron*, a bisque-colored pottery water container with a narrow spout at one end from which, in the Spanish manner, one drank from a jet of water without ever touching the *poron*. The water was cool and the gesture courteous. After this I was surprised by how easily he accepted my presence. The *Hungaros* I had grown up with had also been horsedealers and with a reluctant admiration he told me about their skills. His own father had been one of the greatest horsedealers among the *Gitanos* of Spain. "He could fix a horse," he said, "in such a manner that he lasted through the entire day of the fair, but the great ones among the *Hungaros* could fix horses to last a whole week!"

I told him how after my release from captivity I had lived with them mostly around Madrid until I had left for England to resume wartime service. At that time I had gotten to know some *Gitanos* but neither very well nor intimately.

"Gitanos have become *apayado*," he said with a scowl. They have become assimilated, more like Spaniards than like *Gitanos*. "We are *Gitano Gitano*," he said, no longer on the defensive. "We have never settled down. We are more like you, *Hungaros*. You travel the world but we are trapped here. Because you speak *Romani*, you can go anywhere and

join brothers abroad. We have lost our language. Very few of the younger people speak *Calo*. My brothers and I travel to the horsefairs in Estramadura and Andalusia but our home is on the steppes of Estramadura. The other *Gitanos* are different from us. They lived with and among the *payos* in the *chabolas*, the slums. The *Guardia Civil* hate us and we hate them too. They make our life hard. They hound us. They harass us."

He stretched, stood up, and with a gesture invited me to follow him. We squatted by the crackling fire I had noticed earlier half hidden behind a cart. A young woman gave us spoons and we started to eat. She had wild, uncombed, black hair and thick, luxurious eyebrows that gave her a certain sultry, savage charm. We ate chunks of sausage simmered in a sauce of onion and chickpeas, eaten from the cooking pot and washed down with water from the *poron*.

After the impromptu meal, we walked back to the horsemarket together ostensibly to meet other *Gitanos* from his group.

I had not attended a horsefair since the war. The Gypsies I lived with ever after had become motorized with the exception of those roaming the U.S.S.R. and the Balkans.

The yearly horsefair in Sevilla was an important event attended by both gentry and farmers from all over the nine provinces.

There was a section reserved for the sale of mules and donkeys, and for workhorses and another one for saddle and riding horses. It was with a deep nostalgia that I observed the familiar activities, vividly remembering my own horsedealing days in my teens. I felt as if I were back in the 1930s.

The plain was hot and dusty. Taking me by the arm, and with a display of familiarity, Regalito took me to meet his relatives. He introduced me as a *Hungaro*, "one of us." They were shabbily dressed but a fierce and proud lot, confident and at ease. They looked like a different breed from the *Gitanos* I had seen before, most of whom were guitarists, singers, or dancers. We shook hands all around and at Regalito's invitation we went to have a drink at a nearby drinking booth. To my surprise, he ordered beer in preference to wine, and throughout that afternoon it was beer we drank.

At intervals one of the men would excuse himself and leave to attend to business, or another man would join our group. There was on the part of the Spaniards an unmistakable antagonism which the *Gitanos* pretended not to notice, or rather which they countered by asserting their equality with a swaggering display of *machismo,* which I can only translate as total masculinity. It brought to my mind the description of the *Gitanos* a Spaniard once gave me as "the most despised and haughty of races." They were haughty all right.

Many of the men of Regalito's group owned horses and mules, but some acted as middlemen between non-Gypsy buyers and sellers. One local *Gitano* who bought and sold donkeys was very popular with the *payos,* for whose benefit he acted out roles of comedy or sometimes outrageous villainy. His performances were punctuated by the unearthly sound of a braying donkey.

I, who shortly before had fallen in love with Sevilla and had deeply identified with Spain, watched all around us Spanish faces hardened in contemptuous sneers. I found myself implacably drawn to these *Gitanos* and sided with them against the *payos*. The *Gitanos* loudly addressed me as *primo,* cousin, wilfully provoking the others.

A young cousin of Regalito put a high-strutting steed through his paces, running up and down to demonstrate the animal's qualities, raising clouds of dust. The horse's tail was standing perkily erect, it's neck arched and its head bobbing. It had a silky shine and was superbly groomed.

I lingered, unable to tear myself away. Among the horsedealing *Gitanos* I had a feeling of buoyant physical well-being. It was a much needed spartan antidote to what I suddenly saw as a surfeit of both animation and monotony of the *Feria*.

For these *Gitanos* I felt a kinship that verged on the illusion of being understood, a feeling I had only known before among the *Lowara*.

It was getting late and many people were leaving. We ordered a last round of drinks *"para despedir nos,"* as a parting.

Young boys brought the horses and mules. Some stallions moved sideways restlessly. They collided with others alongside. They reared while others stepped aside. A young *Gitano* mounted one of the high-strung horses and, holding several others by long ropes attached to their halters, took off riding hard. Amid farewells the entire cavalcade rode away in a whirlwind of dust. The last parting sound was a loud whinny.

Regalito, several other men, and I walked back, past the camp, to a nearby *venta,* or country inn. We ordered a bottle of wine and had some *bocadillos,* snacks.

Now that the horsefair was over, the men were more relaxed and conversation resumed and pleasantly expanded. A half-drunken Spaniard rudely asked them to perform a song and dance, but he was ignored. He kept up a patter of mumbled disparaging remarks while an invalid boy with a white skin and a bitter smile listened amused. Several older men playing cards at a table voiced their annoyance at the presence of "those" people. There was not only the cantankerous drunk venting his animosity, but there was also a mentality that allowed it to happen and gave it tacit support. I was troubled by something in the air, something unseen, undefined, something ugly just beyond the grasp. The *Cale,* as the *Gitanos* call themselves, reacted by perhaps too obvious an indifference. The demand for song and dance carried an insulting undertone and I had difficulty concealing my impatience.

We ate and drank and conversed and after a while we walked out and went to yet another *venta*. A number of *Gitanos* we had met earlier in the day had already gathered here. The place was much poorer but the atmosphere was less cold or hostile. Like the other customers, the Gypsies were poorly dressed but whenever the turn came for one of them to treat, he payed with high denomination bank notes peeled off from a thick wad kept loose in his trouser pocket.

"Hungaro," Regalito's brother suddenly began, addressing me by the generic name of my tribe rather than by my name. It sounded formal, as if, through me as a witness, he was addressing all nomadic Gypsies abroad. *"Hungaro, tienes buena sombra,"* you have a good shadow, which I interpreted as "you are one with insight." His voice was coaxing where his stance was theatrical but, instinctively, I sensed an act of friendship

and I trusted him.

"Those of your relatives who lived here in Spain have left. They know a bad shadow hangs over Spain. Tell them that a few *Gitano Gitanos* still survive in isolated areas and in mountain wildernesses. The others are rotting away." He spoke with a somber lyrical exuberance and a richness of language, of which, had I not known the accomplished poetry of their *cante*, I would not have thought them capable. It was also obvious he was over-dramatizing. We had been drinking together for many hours, and if he seemed suddenly a little exalted, I felt mellow and tolerant of his excess.

"The *Gitanos* are rotting away. They are driven outcast. They have no other place of rest but the hospital, the jail, or the grave. A few talented ones peddle romantic illusions but they allow it to corrupt their souls as well. Easy living dulls their desire for freedom. Is it not the beautiful bird that gets caged first? Others seek the meaning of life in fighting the bulls or in the experience of crime. The *Guardia Civil* will run the Gypsies into the ground. They will machine gun all of them. They will separate man from woman, child from mother, and lock them up in jails. The *payos* will cheer them on in erasing the blot, the *Gitanos*, from the National Honor. It will serve to instruct our boys in fear as once they were instructed in courage. The *Guardia Civil* hates us because we are weak. They hate us because we suffer. They hate us because we are oppressed. I tell you there is a shadow over Spain. There is a shadow over *Gitanos*."

We walked back and forth in the gathering dusk.

"If you stay in Spain you will find many of my race but most of them have become *apayado*, Hispanized. You will find them in the *chabolas*, in the slum districts, in back alleys, in the *baracones*, in the *casitas bajas*, wherever live the poor and the voiceless. Some remain conscious of their chains. For those there is hope. A very few, in exchange for a limited freedom, have risen to wealth and, with wealth, to respectability. The *Cale* are dispersed in touchy factions and some of them have, no doubt, a high opinion of themselves. But all the same they are rotting

away." The recitation was monotonous when Regalito fell in with the lyrics of a *cante* about love gone away:

No te deseo más castigar	I do not wish you greater punishment
no te deseo más daño	I do not wish you greater harm
está dormiendo con otro	you lie beside another man
y de mi está acordando	and all the while you think of me

He put his arm through mine as we walked. In a low raucous voice he sang to me, illustrating or paraphrasing in *coplas* what his brother had said.

"Ante de ser mujer mala, ha sio mujer de bie," or as William Blake said, every harlot was a virgin once.

We walked on and his brother took over the singing, changing the meaning and the mood with the words of a different *cante*: "His love turned to hate," he sang in urgent, driving rhythm and with his horsedealer's cane he tapped out the accompaniment, and "his hate drove him mad." Just as great love is inarticulate, great sorrow is mute. The melodies they sang at first sounded deceptively simple but were most intricate, with difficult, unexpected changes of rhythm. The words in their intense spareness, full of echoes of things that were not said and with the imminence of revelations that never came, were evocative, indirect, disarmingly illusive, almost related to Haiku. To them, the meaning was obvious and the singing came from an inner necessity, more appropriate for the occasion than the spoken words.

Regalito clasped me in an emotional but manly embrace. *"Todo está dicho,"* all has been said, he whispered hoarsely. His brother put his arm around my shoulders in silence. Abruptly they walked away from me into the night.

For a moment I felt lost and dizzy. I strained to hear for a little longer the sound of their retreating steps. Then that, too, faded away. I felt very lonely and filled, on account of the *Cale*, with a sense of tragedy and pessimism.

These semi-nomadic horsedealing *Gitanos* of Spain were in spirit closer to the *Rom* than I had dared to anticipate. They had the same intense, passionate urge to express their feelings and were equally reticent to analyze these emotions in words. Rather than rational or descriptive, their structure was purely poetic, expressionistic, eluding the grasp of the Western mind, yet a powerful catalyst to the imagination. The experience had been intense, impossible to forget. I had a sense of completion and at the same time, inexplicably, a sense of beginning. It left me groping for a deeper reality, the extent of which I could not then grasp. I knew it had been an act of friendship rare among men, not so much a meeting of minds as of hearts, which nothing that had preceded it made me feel I deserved. It was a present from those called haughty and despised because they chose to be free. They were men antagonistic to any authority or to any control.

I walked away and followed the Guadalquivir, past the squad Torre del Oro, and, after a short walk, into the warrenlike old quarters.

The *Feria* was still on for one last day and the city resounded with the infectious gaiety of *Sevillanas*. Night clapping echoed through the dark streets, stopping abruptly in admirable unison. With a violent throw of the dice, the merrymaking for me had lost its allure and become hollow. It was like Dante's return among the indifferent.

I had not noticed earlier how the *Guardia Civil* was everywhere. I saw signs offensive to the government painted on the walls. A few had already been painted out with the fury and gusto of the best of the first generation U.S. action painters: the writing on the wall now invisible. I was moved by the visual beauty of the raw power of it. The neat little swastica as a generic signature, added at the bottom by those whose mission it was to obliterate whatever had been painted there before, pleased me less. Defacing walls with political slogans against the authorities was illegal, and as such was punishable by up to six years in jail. Almost simultaneously with these impressions I became aware of the disproportionate number of blind, maimed, and crippled.

Sevilla was one of the gayest cities on the surface. The *Semana Santa* started as a state

funeral, the *Feria* ended the spring rites as a *bachanalia*. If Sevilla—enticing, yet withdrawn, wrapped in secret, rich and tragic dreams—belonged to the centennial past, the *Cale* belonged, without a doubt, to the millennial one.

Chapter 4
Historical Facts

Some historical facts and dates about the Gypsies in Spain.

SINCE I had arrived in Spain, I had been too stimulated to sleep when I came home in the early morning hours; instead I reread William H. Prescot's *Conquest of Mexico and Peru*. After meeting Regalito and his people, I went through notes and photocopies of documents I had gathered about early historical records of the *Gitanos* in Spain as general background material—from the first, I had intended postponing reviewing this material because I sought empathy rather than statistics.

The arrival of the Gypsies was first recorded at the time of the unification of Spain under Isabella and Ferdinand (the Catholic Kings), the conquest of Granada from the Moors (culminating the many centuries of the Reconquest), and the discovery of America that developed Spain into a world power.

Their appearance in the Western world had been sporadically reported as early as 1370 in Corfu, in 1407 in Hildesheim. Then in 1422 in Bale, Switzerland, they were reported to have arrived with a troupe of one hundred horses. In 1427 they arrived in Paris and created a stir. They crossed the

Pyrenees, and in 1477 we find them in Barcelona.

The drive of Islam—repulsed in Spain at great expense—threatened Europe in the guise of the Ottoman Empire, and the Jews everywhere were persecuted at the time the Gypsies penetrated the West.

Sensing the temper of the time and cleverly evaluating the credulity of Europeans of that era, they claimed to be pilgrims from a mythical Little Egypt. Pilgrimages to Rome and Santiago de Compostella were at an apogee; pilgrims were welcomed and generously assisted. The archives recorded the arrivals of small groups led by Duque Andreas, Thomas, Earl of Egypt, Don Johan de Egipte Menor. All these groups were led by chieftains claiming titles of captain, count, knight, or voivode. They rode on horseback and possessed hunting dogs' clear attributes of undisputable nobility. They were said to carry letters of protection from impressive sponsors like the Roman Catholic Pope, Holy Roman Emperor Sigismund, and from Alfonso the Fifth of Aragon.

The reasons the Gypsies gave for their pilgrimage varied widely, grew, and adapted to prevalent local socio-religious conditions. Some claimed their Egyptian ancestors had failed to succor Mary, Joseph, and the Infant Jesus when they fled Herod's vengeance; others claimed to expiate the curse put on their ancestors for having forged the nails with which Our Lord was crucified; still others went back to the prophecies of the Book of Ezekiel (29.12) "I will scatter the Egyptians among all nations and will disperse them." Other groups did penance for their ancestors' claimed apostasy under the duress of Moslem rule. Other Gypsy groups developed endless variations upon similar themes. All of them stated the period of wandering and penance to be seven years, but it was unclear on which date this started; it seemingly went on forever.

During the earlier migratory period, the Egyptians had been received with tolerance, often with generosity. However, their real, or alleged, riotous behavior, their begging and pilfering, their fortune-telling and practice of magic, and their dances, unseemly for Christian pilgrims, led to their ostracism. They were declared outlaws, that is, they could be killed with impunity by all, and

they were banished from many kingdoms. With rare tolerant intervals, the cruel persecutions went on unabated for nearly half a millennium.

In 1499, under the Edict of Medina del Campo, the Catholic Kings of Spain proclaimed that "to contain the Gypsy scourge, they were cursed to be destroyed."

They were given sixty days to leave the kingdom. If found after this time, they would receive one hundred whiplashes before being forcibly expelled. If caught again within the boundaries of the kingdom, they were to be taken into slavery. In 1539, Charles V condemned the Gypsies found in Spain to six years of forced labor.

Between 1528 and 1598 alone, more than thirty repressive legal measures were taken against them, an average of one every other year.

The necessity for the endless reapplications of the law of expulsion, under increasingly severe penalties, only proves their apparent ineffectiveness.

Those allowed to remain, under special license, were forbidden to wander, to speak their language, to wear their distinctive costume, to trade in horses, to work as blacksmiths, to tell fortunes, or to congregate. They were forced to live in special ghettoes, *Gitanerias*.

Chapter 5
Coria del Rio

Return to my family's ancestral estate in Coria del Rio.

THE time had come for me to go to Coria del Rio where my father grew up and where my grandfather, and his father before him, had owned the ancestral *finca*. I longed to be outside in the country. I longed for pastoral dignity and the wide-open land of simple-hearted people.

I followed the Guadalquivir downstream, passing the spot, now deserted, where I had visited the *Cale*. After a few miles the paved road gave way to a dirt track deeply rutted by ox carts. Blossoming orchards alternated with groves of gray-green olive trees, gnarled and fantastically twisted, and silvery patches of almond trees in full bloom. The road passed through a string of Andalusian *pueblos* with low, square buildings, flat-roofed and covered with thick coats of whitewash until all angles were rounded off. The sun was burning and dogs sleeping. Besides looking picturesque, behind the stubborn misconception about life here being wonderfully simple and assured, the *pueblos* exuded a general air of backwardness and decay. They were somnolent and conservative and nothing ever happened but death and marriages, good and bad olive years. This was the deep south of Spain in its unambiguous actuality where prevailed the oldest interpretation of religion and feudalism. It was an old stationary world of fixed dogma and the disparity between the rich and the destitute was awesome. The light was implacable, all outlines were clear and there were no shadows.

These southern *pueblos* were strangely haunting with a gone-away feeling and a disconsolate resigned forsakenness, despite the lingering pungency of the past.

We passed peasants seated sideways on mules. Invariably they greeted us. And we passed long lines of donkeys heavily laden.

We traveled through stretches covered with low shrubs and abundant wild flowers, or patches of vivid red earth contrasting with the blue sky.

A few years before, at the age of ninety, my father had moved to the Canary Islands where, with my mother, he had made his home. Recently he had expressed a wish to return to Coria del Rio, and we had agreed to meet and spend Easter together in Sevilla. We had planned to spend Holy Week there, and after visiting the village where he spent his childhood and early manhood, to go on the pilgrimage to El Rocio together. When the time came, his health was not up to it and consequently I had come alone on this secular pilgrimage.

My younger sister had prepared the way by correspondence with the proper authorities and discovered the existence of Don Juan Leal.

In Coria del Rio, after I introduced myself at the *ayuntamiento,* a municipal guard was sent along to escort me to the house of Don Juan Leal Pereira, who in the old days had been the *encargado,* or manager, of my grandfather's *finca.* Don Juan's father had held the same position before him.

The house where he lived on the main street was built in brick contrasting with its neighbors' whitewashed adobe ones. The windows were barred with handsome wrought iron grilles in the fashion of Andalusia. The municipal guard, a man in late middle age and unusually reticent for an Andalusian, knocked loudly on the solid, nail-studded front door. In an overly loud voice, as if speaking to the deaf, he commanded that the door be opened immediately, and at the same time he gave out accurate information about the visitor, me, I had no inkling he was capable of. Here was Don Juan Batista, son of Don Eugenio who was the son of Don Jorge, he of the *finca.* Then, without waiting for a possible answer, he started to knock again insistently. I felt embarrassed and at the same time like royalty itself. The heavy, nail-studded door opened wide. An elderly, somewhat overweight woman, well dressed and with magnificent hair, bade me welcome with the courteous saying of Spain: *"Esta casa es suya,"* consider this house as yours. She sounded deferent and at the same time familiar.

Inside it was cool and dark. The wooden floor was well-scrubbed and there was an abundance of devotional pictures. At first glance I recognized the Virgin of the Macarena and the Paloma Blanca of El Rocio. The furniture was banal and conventional.

Don Juan Leal emerged from the shadow of a darkened ground-floor bedroom where he had been resting. He was a tall, robust man, with a healthy complexion. I later learned he was nearly ninety years old. His hair was dark gray and short. He wore a dark suit and an impeccably white shirt. He, too, bade me welcome with the same combination of familiarity and deference as his daughter had before him. I could not help thinking of it as befitting a trusted retainer greeting a returning feudal landowner after a long absence.

He asked me in an avuncular, chiding tone, softened by the obvious warmth of his entire attitude: "By your permission, Don Juan, what took you so long coming home?" I had never before been in Coria del Rio, and, I had to remind myself, my father had left, never to return, sixty odd years ago.

Don Juan Leal did not expect an answer, this was only by way of making me aware of how much I belonged here in my ancestral home. He went right on telling me about Don Jorge—the paternal grandfather I had never known because he died before I was born—as if he had spoken to him the day before. "This is Don Jorge's favorite brandy," he said, using the present tense, when his daughter brought in the decanter and put it before him on the table. She brought him a bottle of Jerez explaining, by way of apology, that for the last few years her father had not been well and was not allowed to drink by doctor's orders. He winked and smiled tolerantly.

Instead of inquiring how long I intended to stay, he gave orders that my room be put in order "right away," ignoring my protests. Because of his age, he no longer kept a riding horse. "I gave it away to my grandson three years ago," but a good horse would be provided for me, "right away." Again my protest was passed over simply, as good form prescribed. "If only we had known you would be coming, all these details would have been taken care of." My apologies for arriving unannounced were brushed over. "You are here, con Dios, and all is well."

Don Juan Leal called for his walking stick and hat and, against his daughter's protests that he was not well and my own objections, insisted on walking with me to the old finca.

The neighbors had apparently already been informed of my visiting Don Juan Leal, "the grandson of Don Jorge who had come all the way from Nueva York." The men stood in front of their houses, the women inside their doorways, to wish me welcome to Coria del Rio. It made me feel like the return of the prodigal son of the Old Testament and I had to remind myself again and

again that my father had left this village more than half a century ago.

Most people were obviously too young to have known either my father or my grandfather, but Don Juan Leal explained that everybody knew about them. I wondered what kind of a man Don Jorge, my grandfather, must have been to be remembered so long afterward with so much affection. I was unwilling to admit, because the concept was so alien to me, that here in Coria del Rio time had stood still. And it was to take me a long time to realize that, as impossible as it sounded, this was simply the case.

The finca, or rather what was left of it, stood at the edge of the Guadalquivir. It still was a majestic, massive two-story stone building with a cavernous entrance gate built to accommodate coaches and horses. It led to a colonnaded inner courtyard.

As a child, I had seen a painting on glass of the family finca surrounded by extensive orange groves, as seen from across the river.

The Guadalquivir had eaten the land away, "se lo comió," as Don Juan Leal put it plastically; and with the land the orange groves had gone. Part of the finca was now used as a flour depot and another part had become a furniture factory. Don Juan pointed out to me, with the pride of an archeologist, which parts were "authentic," that is, from Don Jorge's time, and which had been added on or altered more recently. By more recently, he meant in the last fifty years. Each meticulous description was prefaced by "as you no doubt know," or "as your father must have told you," only to remind me of my ignorance of my family's past and the extent to which my father himself had changed after he left Spain, omitting to inculcate me with his own heritage.

More and more I came to appreciate how my father's love for Spain and all things Spanish was essentially prismatic. As an artist, he had created the form of his desire. Presently I saw the extent to which this world was recognizably his own. His nostalgia for paradise lost, distilled further by exile, had fed his art and was its roots. It dawned on me, too, that one day perhaps my children might ask themselves that same question about my love for the nomadic Rom with whom, in my youth, I had lived idyllic years; and they, in turn, may misconstrue why I ever gave it up. Throughout my youth I had wondered why my father, with his passionate love for Spain, chose voluntary exile in Flanders, but I had failed to formulate this clearly enough to ask him.

In Coria del Rio, I sensed, like seldom before, the impossible return to the past; my father's to Spain, or my own to the world of the *Rom*. We both had been away too long. I had wanted for so long to walk here, where he grew up, and where before him, his father did. I felt lonelier now, being here without him.

Don Juan Leal insisted in taking me all over Coria del Rio. He insisted on showing me, and explaining to me, every little detail he remembered. When I objected that he should not tire himself out too much, he only answered: "This is the last time I can share all this with anyone who cares. Times are changing. Few old-timers survive. If you had come last year you would still have seen *la Murilla* [the name literally meant the Moorish one]. Would she have loved to meet Don Jorge's grandson. She was his—his housekeeper, and she loved him and spoke about him until she died in her late nineties."

He showed me the two walnut trees, now black and still, my grandfather Don Jorge had planted; and he showed me where, before they had been destroyed to make way for the new asphalt road, the caves of the Gypsies had been.

Proudly he showed me the *paseo*, a short shaded grove along the Guadalquivir. It was paved and had well-tended patches of flowers, and in the afternoon most of the inhabitants of Coria del Rio came here to walk and to see each other. Here young men and young girls, endlessly walking past each other, day after day, week after week, exchanged glances, which, in time, might lead to the customary, formal evening visits—the girl in her window behind the iron grille, the man outside in the street, observed by all.

"Coria del Rio has maintained her standing, but there are many *despoblados,* dead villages, all over Andalusia. Young men go to work in Germany and the women go to Barcelona, or even to France, to work as maids. They don't come back here. Soon only we, the old ones, will be left—and the Gypsies."

Chapter 6
Cave Dwellers

In search of the "true Gypsies" I stumble upon the warrenlike labyrinth of present-day cave dwellers but fail to meet Gypsies.

IT was in search of the true, untamed, uncontaminated *Cale*, in search of the scattered few wild ones, of the hidden remnants, that one day I left the sultry heat and the intoxicating perfume of Sevilla and the amenities that urban dwellers take for granted. I left behind me the oasis of orchards and the groves of orange, olive, and almond trees with the occasional patch of flowering apricots, to enter a wasteland of silence and unrelenting sun.

At first I passed exhausted, fallow land. The soil was red and smoldered in the heat, studded here and there with cactus and prickly pears. Farther along, the red soil turned yellow and there was an abundance of rocks. Intermittently, herds of black goats rushed around and leaped about. The landscape had a barren, parched nakedness. We were traveling enveloped in a haze of dust. The road twisted and climbed until we came upon the gray, silent grandeur of the Sierra Nevada. With their bases hidden by low, rutted hills that looked like a cloudbank, they seemed to be hanging in the sky. A gigantic snow-covered wall loomed over the arid steppe. High overhead, an eagle soared, a prey in its claws.

We arrived at the ancient city of Guadix.

It was a listless, sleepy, dull market town. Something about it reminded me uncannily of either Skopje, in Yugoslav Macedonia, or of Central Turkey. It was dominated by an eighteenth-century, red sandstone cathedral and had a handsome arcaded square. In Roman times it had been a center of silver-mining.

Trouble began when I asked directions to the Cañada de la Garcia. No one had ever heard of it. There was much shaking of heads. I asked for the Barrio de Santiago. "No, no, definitely not here." Tentatively, I then asked where the Gypsies lived. They stared blankly or walked away shrugging their shoulders. One old man, intrigued by my interest in low life or possibly just more helpful than the others, pointed in the direction of the Sierras, but he could not resist mumbling some warning against going there.

I settled down at a local inn and had coffee and a snack. Unhurriedly, I watched the activities in the square to get into the local mood and rhythm. I also hoped to engage in conversation more reliable informants. There were the usual donkeys, mules, horses, and rows of trucks. The people looked very poor, stolid, and unfriendly—at least in comparison to Sevilla.

My dilemma was eventually solved simply by hiring one of the few local taxicabs. For the price of the fare, and the hope of an adequate tip, he drove me up the hill, north of the city, and without any hesitation, straight to the cave city. His only words of caution to me were that "son gente humilde," those living up there are humble people, or in other less reticent words: extremely poor. He said it only to prepare me for what I would see and to appeal to my sense of tolerance.

The road soon stopped and we drove on over a narrow, rough track definitely not intended for cars. The wheels lost their grip. We skidded from side to side and raised clouds of choking dust that penetrated the closed windows. I marveled at the driver's mad unconcern and expected the car to break down, to smash into the rock wall, or to tumble down over the narrow edge into the ravine.

The forbidding setting and the special conditions under which we traveled reminded me of an equally arduous trip in Nepal where we had come upon an ominous sign warning that "beyond this point road no longer jeep-able"!

I reflected there were places more easily reached by mule than by car but the driver drove on unperturbed by my misgivings. "Aqui en España . . .," here in Spain, he explained between bumps and shocks, "We know how to drive."

It was difficult to imagine a large population, as I had been led to expect, living anywhere hereabout. The place was at best the setting for a few shepherds or an hermit monk.

With much roaring of the motor, we climbed to the top of a low hill from where the rock-strewn track dipped down again. And there, through the dusty windshield, I saw opening up before me, in all directions, the sunbaked, fantastic region of cave dwellings. The roar of the car ceased abruptly and with it the lurching motion. We waited for the dust to settle down somewhat before we got out. The silence was ominous; I was transfixed by the lunar strangeness and eerie desolation. It was like an otherworldly hallucination of giant petrified fungi, extensively perforated into endless cliff dwellings; a geological accident pierced with openings.

It was warm and completely windless, and the hum of insects was reassuring. The cave openings were like empty sockets in a giant skull. I saw a warrenlike labyrinth of deep, barren gullies and of narrow rocky ledges and paths plunging down, or in counter rhythm rising, into an intricate multilevel pattern fanning out from this center spot.

There was not a human being to be seen anywhere. The dry, deceptive light seemed to distort scale, distances and proportions. At first the entrance holes to the caves looked too small to accommodate humans. The very next moment, they seemed to change in scale, fit for giants. There were no trees or plants, animals, or known objects as reference for size. All life seemed suspended in centuries of silence.

Each lair was on a different level, partly facing different direction. No two caves were alike. Each pinnacle, cliff, or cone, shaped by erosion and water, was distinct. Everywhere strangely shaped, whitewashed contraptions sprouted, archaic survivals that proved to be a veritable harvest of chimneys. A wisp of smoke told me the place, deep in the bowels of the earth, was inhabited.

Out of the startling profusion of unfamiliar, angular, jagged shapes I started to distinguish telling details: a vine-covered trellised porch, a small stack of hay, a black hen, a man's shirt drying in the still, warm air. At the lower levels, the areas around the entrances had been smoothed out to form a façade and were whitewashed. I scaled the summit of a nearby hillock to find more ravines, more red cliffs, more strange habitats. Surrealistically, a donkey was tethered to a chimney of the cave at the level below. I discovered an inner courtyard formed by nature and erosion. A woman dressed in black was milking a goat. I was deeply affected by the visual, architectonic beauty of the barrio and wondered what kind of men, women, and children lived here and how the stark environment, and living under the ground, would affect these modern troglodytes.

Straight ahead of me, standing motionless, on top of another small hill, was a man with a dog at his heels, scanning the horizon. When he noticed me, he waved with a restrained, dignified gesture. He motioned to me to join him. At first I hesitated, unsure of his motives, against my habit, instinctively distrustful. I came down into the ravine, and following the directions signaled to me by his articulate hand movements, I managed to join him after a difficult climb.

He swept the horizon in a generous gesture of his outstretched arm to share with me what apparently even to him was the beauty and awesomeness of the world he lived in. From the top of his hill, I saw endless further hills with innumerable caves. They were carved out of cliffs and hills and they had similar mushroom-chimneys and narrow ledges leading to the various levels. The hills were of soft argillaceous sandstone. Sometimes they were covered with the thinnest patches of earth that made them, in the surrounding barrenness, look like quilts of down. I saw a solitary blossoming wild fig tree. The man pointed out to me different features of the fantastic landscape. He was very much at ease, neither hostile, cowed, nor in any way interested in material gain. Since I had bothered to come this far, he wanted to share with me what he knew and loved, and that was all. I can never forget the deeply moving, grandiose forlornness of the Barrio de Santiago standing between earth and sky. I answered his question of where I hailed from, trying as best I could to describe to him, in this present setting, what I knew must sound to him as unnatural and exotic as his world did to me.

I accepted the hospitality he offered me. We came down from our observation post. After a short, precarious walk along narrow, crumbling gullies he invited me into his cave home. He pushed aside an earth-colored blanket that served as a door and briskly clapped together his hands to inform whoever was inside of our presence.

In contrast to the heat outside, the temperature inside was pleasantly cool. I was surprised at the spaciousness inside, which, from the outside, I had not suspected. We sat down on low wicker stools. He had no wine, he said, but offered me milk from a brown earthenware bowl. It had the hard, wild, sweetish taste of goatmilk I had forgotten since my childhood. He offered me a piece of hard corn bread and some small purple onions.

The ceilings were arched and arched passageways led into other open spaces. I was reluctant to define them as rooms. Sleeping alcoves and cupboards were hollowed out of the rocks. Despite the heat outside, a charcoal brazier burned in a corner. There was electric light. He told me that some of the caves had running water and a few even had a telephone.

In answer to my questions, he said he did not know how many people lived here in the barrio but they were many, many thousands. "Here we live together, but from here you can walk for hours in any direction and find inhabited caves. There are also many other barrios." He recited on: "There is Benalua and Marchar and Graena and Purullena, Loja, Motril, Padul, Montefrio, Iznalloz, and Salobuenas." I had assumed that he lived here isolated and cut off from the outside world, to discover that he was an integral part of another world, unsuspected and therefore unexplored by us. I knew, or had heard of, some cave villages in Almanzora, in the province of Almeria, in La Guardia in New Castile, in Calatayud, southwest of Zaragoza, in the heart of Aragon. I knew of some right near Madrid where refugees were housed temporarily.

I asked him where the Gypsies lived. He said there were only very few of them living here, in the more primitive quarters near the summit. "No, people who live here in the better section are all good Spaniards. The *Gitanos* have their own cave city in Granada. That is where you will find them. Not here. But in the Sacromonte, where they sing and dance." I took leave of him. "May God be with you," he said in parting. I climbed to where the "more primitive quarters" started.

I had until then, perhaps somewhat naively, taken for granted that a few Gypsies lived in these caves and in this fashion; I had been reluctant to admit that in the twentieth century, and for that matter in Spain, to all practical purposes in Europe, Spanish citizens lived under such conditions. They were not even refugees displaced by some natural disaster, political or economic crisis, eventually to be resettled. My host in the cave had stated with calm emphasis: "We have lived here yesterday, we live here today— we will live here forever."

The ledges here were narrower, more deeply eroded, and more inaccessible than in the other parts. On my way up I passed the entrance of a cave that looked deserted. The main opening looked like a gaping mouth, and several irregularly-placed, smaller openings, which must have been windows, looked like eyes. In the harsh shade of one of the holes, I saw an old wizened woman staring at me with suspicious eyes.

The path ended near the top and there were no more caves. Idly I climbed to the highest point to survey from there the area I had come through. Instead, and as if looking into Alice's looking glass, I saw over the rim a hollow the size of a large stone quarry, but less deep, with rows upon rows of holes at irregular and different levels. It was like a huge ant hill in brooding monochromes.

Unable to resist the lure of the labyrinth, and encouraged to do so by the lack of attention and absence of hostility, I stepped down into this secluded valley. The moment was timeless and my mood strictly contemplative.

Unexpectedly, children in indescribable rags collected from everywhere. They came running, sure-footed and agile, with roars of delight. Too late I realized that this section, difficult enough to reach, would prove even more difficult to approach or penetrate on account of its children running wild in gangs. They were shouting, pestering, fighting among themselves, like young unruly animals. Any moment I could, and by force of circumstances I ought to, become their target.

When I grew up as a child among the *Rom,* in the Balkans, I had often, unabashed and with a special joy, participated in similar harassment of any intruder into our camp space. The adult *Rom,* if they did not actively encourage it, at least tolerated our rambunctious games at the expense of outsiders. It created an invisible, though almost impassable, protective wall around their private domain.

For me it was too late to retreat. Flight was unseemly, or worse. Without any other choice I ventured in, but with few illusions. Out of a hole, in the otherwise solid group, an adult came toward me. The onrushing children slowed their momentum and were satisfied to cluster about me just a few paces away. Waiting. It was a vivacious young woman, bewitchingly beautiful. She was dressed in tatters and unbelievably dirty. She exuded an irrepressible, contagious vitality. How could human beings living under such difficult conditions have, or retain, such insatiable hunger for life? The contrast between the Spaniards and the *Gitanos,* between those I had seen living in the lower, "better," part of the caves and those living in the inaccessible "more primitive" section, was shocking. The entrances to the caves below were whitewashed and showed signs of care compared to the unkept appearance of the holes in which, like wild animals, the *Gitanos* had their lairs. To judge by the number of children here, as numerous it seemed as the flies, and the absence of them in the other part, the *Gitanos* were miraculously prolific, or their infant mortality rate negligible. Perhaps, it occurred to me, the Spanish children were attending school.

Whatever the conditions under which they were born and grew up, the *Gitano* children were far less apathetic. Here was no sullen or mute poverty; abundant vitality and filth matched each other, or perhaps canceled each other out.

The young *Gitana,* fresh as dawn, firm of flesh and bewitchingly beautiful as I ever saw, interrupted my speculations. With a bright, engaging smile, which further disarmed me and disposed me in her favor, she directed at me a flow of obscenities, to the exultant joy of the cheering mob of small children. Taken aback, I tried to talk to her but she was as pugnacious and unapproachable as she had shown herself unpredictable. Humbled, I walked back the way I had come, followed all the way by peals of clear, exuberant, even if insolent, laughter.

I drove on to Granada along the new asphalt road that swept at the base of rugged mountain. A few miles further along, rounding a bend, the road passed right through the middle of the cave city of Purullena. The caves opened up on either side, right at road level. They looked well-kept, and the hills out of which they were carved were less eroded, less wild and grotesquely shaped than those of Guadix. The skyline was almost flat. It gave an impression of peacefulness. Several caves bordering on the asphalt had displays of Hispano-Moorish ceramic plates and the deep bowls typical of Granada for sale. For a brief moment I thought I had hit upon a pottery center, but closer scrutiny showed them to have been massproduced. Purullena was comparatively small, but what made it sensational was the blatant contrast between the almost prehistoric and the technologically advanced: the truck alongside the cave entrance.

I drank some strong, black coffee at a local inn and bought some bread, fruit, and wine. Then I left the roadside and went into the village proper. There was more visible activity here. Poverty seemed less extreme. I learned that most of the inhabitants worked as day laborers in the neighboring beet fields. There were a few dogs and several cats, the presence, or absence, of which I came to appreciate as a fair indicator of the level of subsistence or total poverty. Here again I found the displays of multicolored geraniums familiar to other parts of Andalusia. If Guadix was overwhelming, strange, and somehow inhuman, Purullena was pretty and picturesque. I was therefore surprised when at my approach girls and young women ran inside the caves for shelter. Gnarled old women, perennially dressed in black, stood their ground and remained at the cave entrances as fearless guardians of the hearth.

A troupe of Gypsies, women and children, wandered by in a tight cluster—the Spaniards, I had noticed, walked alone or when two together, they did so a few paces apart from each other—like a flock of sparrows they rushed toward us with much movement and noise.

They surrounded me, half joking, half impudently begging. They were earthy, vivacious, infuriating, and irresistible. The squalid old women in black, who apparently knew them well and addressed them by name, implacably chased them away. They added, making their weary, knowing, tired eyes look wise, *"son mala gente,"* they are bad people. They had lived for generations in the same community but considered them as hereditary enemies. "They are poisoners of wells, witches, *brujas,* and *hecheceras,"* confirming for them the reality of a world of spells, curses, and magic. From the special sting to their words, I could easily imagine outbreaks of mob savagery, during which, to get rid of whatever they did not understand and to protect the illusion of their own innocence, they could simply dismember the aberrants.

A sudden, quick rain shower made the earth, which had stored up the heat of the day, steam. Everybody ran for shelter and I was left alone, exposed as outsiders, perhaps come to do harm. It became chilly, reminding me of the altitude and of the proximity of the Sierra Nevada with its eternal snows. There followed a magnificent sunset, like a great furnace lighting up the whole sky, which I wished I had seen, instead of here, over the cave city of Guadix.

Chapter 7
The Alhambra

The Oriental splendor of the Alhambra.

WE drove through a deserted region of bare rock, deep canyons, and wild gorges, theatrically lit up by the sweep of the headlights, without passing another car on the road. It was late at night when we reached Granada. At first impression, and admittedly at a disadvantage, the city itself looked disappointing. It was night, and I was deeply affected by the caves I had seen that day. I tried hard not to let this prejudice me against Granada.

I woke up very early but, from past experience, I knew this was not a proper time to go to the Gypsy quarter of Sacromonte, or any other Gypsy encampment anywhere in the world. To while away the time in anticipation of the hour to come, and intensify, if possible, the enjoyment of it, and partly to acquaint myself with Granada and all that it stood for, I walked up the steep wooded hill to the Alhambra.

Everywhere about me was the sound of rushing water and the songs of birds. The shimmering of the new leaves and the damp breath of the trees served as a relevant preamble to the onslaught on all the senses that

I had not expected the Alhambra to be.

At first I was blinded by its weightless magic, its freshness, its exuberant fantasy. From confused exaltation, like a mounting fever, it led into sheer delirium. I felt my heart racing.

The Oriental splendors of the eleventh-century palace—said to have been built by Vizir Yehoseph Ibn Nagralla—enclosed in stern reddish-ocher outer walls, from which its name derives, with their huge square towers—were adequately matched by the delights of the gardens of the Generaliffe, Gennat-al-Arif, the garden of the builders. To what perhaps was the over-refinement of the Moorish palaces, the summer residence and its gardens offered as complement understatement and repose. Unfolding like a dream, intimate, shadowy spaces and quiet retreats, open to the blue sky, were created by tall, melancholy cypress, yew, jasmine, and bougainvillea, combined with the effects of an abundance of wisteria, carpets of violets, fragrant roses, and the constant whisper of flowing water and the spray of endless, unexpected fountains. I think of them as "water gardens" the way I remember from Kyoto, the Ryoanji, and its "stone garden."

My arrival in Granada, as in Sevilla, started with a climax: there was the gracious reveling at the *Feria* in Sevilla; here it was the architectural magnificence of this ephemeral floating world left by the Moors chased from the land. It was difficult to believe that this exotic place had been abandoned for centuries or that it was used as a hospital and at another time had been an asylum for beggars and tramps.

I found it hard to sober up. The day had gone. I walked down the wooded hill, followed by the steady chatter of water flowing abundantly in narrow, man-made conduits down the steep incline. The soft, squashy greenery and the constant babble of water about me everywhere brought back memories of peaceful times in Kyoto. I was filled with the afterglow of what I had seen and felt. It was a background too magnificent to dare imagine mortals living in it.

To assuage my forgotten impatience, and to gain time, I took a taxi to the Albaicin, the old Moorish quarters on top of the hill opposite that on which the Alhambra stood. In the days of the Moors, there the trainers of the hunting hawks had lived. The streets were hot, noisy, and smelly, the crowds dense and vital, bringing back impressions from Samarkand, Mazar-i-Sharif, and Istanbul all in one.

Walking here made the transition easier, I thought, from East to West, from the past to the present, from the Moslem to the Christian world. When I felt sufficiently unwound, I had the driver take me to the Sacromonte.

By the account of almost all the Spaniards I talked to, the Sacromonte was the Eden of Gypsydom, facing the Alhambra. We left the quaint Albaicin, with its superb view of the Alhambra hill, still lit by the last rays of the sun, outlined against the snow-capped peaks of the Sierras. We drove down the steep, narrow street and into the purple dusk. We drove for a long time through a deserted stretch which I had assumed was already Gypsy territory. The driver kept saying "farther down." I started feeling apprehensive. Where were the thousands of Gypsy caves I had so often heard about? "Farther down." I sat back and tried to pretend I was relaxed.

Then we stopped. Neon lights, with their garish phosphorescence, violated the twilight and gave the Sacromonte an unpleasant, incongruous touch of ill-digested modernism. The gleaming, air-conditioned "de luxe Flamenco tour" bus pulled up as we arrived. I protested, refusing to leave the taxicab but the driver was adamant: "This is it. You wanted *Gitanos*. Here they are." As a second thought I decided to do the tourist bit. This was the Zambra of the Camino del Monte. I rationalized that after all it might be at least of interest to see the *Gitanos* the way the tourists saw them, after having been lured here all the way, from wherever they came, by poster and guidebook listings of "touristic interest" in Gypsy caves.

Reluctantly, I paid the extravagantly high tariff and filed into the cave cabaret. The other tourists and I sat on low kitchen chairs. To give it "class" and a synthetic sense of spontaneity and fun, a mandatory glass of cheap sherry was forced upon us. "It is included in the price of admission. You may as well have it." It is unnecessary to further describe the shambles and parody that followed, misleading to the tourists, humiliating to the *Gitanos*.

Much later I was glad that, partly by accident, partly by lack of good judgment, I had been exposed to the other side. No wonder the Gypsy, promoted as a tourist attraction in Spain, often by the officials, came through as a two-dimensional cardboard cut-throat, villain, and thief.

After the show, the taxi driver picked me up to take me back to town. He was not in the least surprised by my bad mood; many tourists reacted that way. "The *Gitanos* are no good. They are thieves, all of them," he consoled me. When time came to settle accounts, the fare was double the sum originally agreed upon. "To the Gypsy caves—at night—double tariff!" He added, then, just in case, "There are many other Zambra-caves, much appreciated by foreigners." When I did not react, he quickly added, "But to tell you the truth, they are all the same." A rhythmic nonsense jingle, the accuracy of which I had dismissed, went *"Granadino, ladron fino,"* Citizen of Granada, clever thief; rather forgotten, involuntarily it came back to haunt me.

Forced by edict to settle, the Gypsies hollowed out caves in the town of Gaudix, high in the desolate Sierras. Their domain is the high, unpaved quarter, with chimneys, like smoking stanchions, set on the plain above. Below, the Spaniards live among proper streets and recognizable habitations. Isolated in this rutted, crágéy wilderness, the two cultures exist symbiotically, unable to separate, unable to integrate.

*Out of prudence, the
Gypsies affect the
trappings of the church.
On their cave walls they
have holy pictures and
artifacts, but spit after a
priest passes.*

The externals of their existence belie the reality and vitality of their ancient heritage.

Chapter 8
Pedro

A descent into the brutal, squalid slums where the Gypsies live. Pedro the working priest. Meeting with Gypsies of various social and economic levels.

THE following day I decided, intrigued by a specific travel brochure entry about admiring Gypsy art and crafts at leisure, to visit the Casa de los Tiros. The book grandly described it as probably the only museum in the entire world devoted to the Gypsies. The Casa de los Tiros was the former palace of the Venegas family, presently housing the local offices of the Ministry of Information and Tourism and, of more interest to me, the Gypsy museum. On display I found a few books on the subject, mostly romantic or sentimental, a small display of photographs, old but of little interest, and as high point a collection of small polychromed figurines depicting Gypsy daily life: a seated Gypsy woman picking lice from the hair of a young boy, and, presumably her husband weaving a basket. Another one showed a Gypsy muledealer bargaining with a *caballero,* while a young Gypsy boy picks the latter's pocket. . . .

Sometime earlier, a casual acquaintance or a friend of a friend had given me the name of a working priest living among the *Gitanos* in Granada. I had politely accepted the well-intentioned information but never intended to follow it up. I wanted to stay clear of official contact, religious or lay. I changed my mind.

At the Plaza Colón I took the local bus number four to the Barrio de la Chana. The guidebooks recommended visits to the Alcaicera, the Moorish silk exchange; the Corral del Carbón, a fine old *caravanserai;* the monastery of San Jeronimo; the cathedral; and the Cartuja (the Carthusian monastery); it never mentioned the Barrio de la Chana.

The bus was overcrowded and it was good to see at close range the average, poor *Granadinos.* I got out at the terminal, La Chana, only to discover the vagueness of my information, as was so often the case in Spain.

The man I was looking for was a *Padre,* a Jesuit priest who lived among the *Gitanos.* I walked around to find my bearings and decide what to do next. I inquired at the nearest church but no, they did not know him. The kindly parish priest sent me to a nearby convent. But no, they did not know either. The door-keeper nun sent along several little girls with eager faces and clean aprons to take me to the orphanage. Maybe they would know. They were nice and helpful and visibly enjoyed the importance of their mission.

The streets were unpaved, the mud deep, and the neighborhood poor. There was extensive construction of public housing, but the building materials looked hopelessly shoddy and inadequate.

The children rang the doorbell of the orphanage and they rang again. I was ready to give up but instead waited with the patience that Spain teaches. After a long time, the door was opened and I had the opportunity to ask Mother Superior about the Jesuit priest I was looking for. She was a saintly-looking woman in her severe, black, monastic uniform, who, as she explained, devoted her life to these poor orphan-girls. She raised her eyebrows, pursed her lips, without making any effort to hide her disapproval. She said, "That Jesuit priest! Sure I know him." Her voice was high and harsh. "He lives near the *frigorifico,* the refrigeration factory, in the *baracones,* the shacks. It is an awful situation! Please don't go there. *Es cosa imunda.* It is a revolting thing. *Gitanos* to begin with are no good. *No vallen nada.* They are not worth anything." I thanked her and left wondering about Christian charity. From her horrified disapproval, I imagined I would find a renegade priest living in sin, involved in some unmentionable scandalous situation.

The neighborhood became gradually more run-down, poverty more visible. I found the *baracones* where the low shacks began in their uniform squalor, with garbage-strewn open spaces, a few feet wide, between them. The mud was ankle deep and reeked of stale urine and human excrement. A badly battered dead rat lay rotting away. It was a brutal, squalid place, fetid and oppressive where lived the scum, the poorest of the poor, the superfluous ones. The shacks were very low and small. Like rows of prison cells they stood, a series of human cages surrounded or hidden by a cinderblock enclosing wall.

I crossed a small open space where the communal privies were, thick with flies, and the outdoor, concrete troughs at which women stood washing clothes. In the middle of a large puddle there was a single water-tap at the end of a pipe protruding from the ground. It provided those of the *baracones* with grossly inadequate water supply, rank from sewage overflow. Children stood around with sad, hungry faces, drowsy eyes, running sores, and little bloated bellies.

The washerwomen called out after me, in contest, ribald commentary and descriptions of sexual imagery and private bodily functions. They did not intend harm or insult. Foulness of tongue, lack of privacy, self-contempt and absence of hope were simply part of the corruptive factors. Nothing unusual, and dog ate dog.

I asked a passing woman if she knew where the *cura,* priest, lived. She seemed surprised by my question. But no, she did not know. No priest could possibly live in such a *porquería,* in such a pigsty! I did not know what to do or whom to ask. Her comment had sounded obvious. How could a priest live here, a Spanish priest at that. Yet the mother superior had said: *"Es cosa imunda. Que no vaya usted."* An outsider, and visibly better off than they were, I attracted too much attention and I knew I could not linger on much longer.

Coming from one of the shacks, drearily similar to all the others, I heard children's voices in unison reciting their lessons. Unbelieving, I listened for a few minutes. To judge from the outside, nothing distinguished it from the others but here, in total limbo, was a school. It was run by several young nuns. In my surprise, I did not even inquire to what Order they belonged and I have no recollection of the type of uniform they wore. Against my wish, I was received as an important guest, an inspector of some sort. What did I want to hear the children recite? Which children in particular did I want to interrogate? All this between stern instructions given in stage whispers. Finally I managed to convince them that all I wanted was to find out from them if they knew a certain *Padre* X. Yes, yes but of course they knew the Jesuit priest, everybody knows him. They were visibly pained by my leaving so soon. "This particular nursery school for destitute children you must understand. . . ." They sent two little girls to accompany me.

Back in the squalor and stench of the alley, it occurred to me belatedly what an oasis their devotion had been able to create, and I wished I had been less preoccupied with my own concern and given them the little time and the little attention they asked for.

The little girls hopped and jumped, trying to avoid mud puddles. They giggled. They saw the alleys the way the gentleman from far away must see them, and in their own childlike ways tried to make amends for what, in any way, they were not responsible: the conditions of their slums.

This time the washerwomen looked up, whispered among themselves, but remained silent. We stopped a few doors away from the public latrines. In singsong voices they declared, *"Aqui viven los curas,"* it is here that the priests live. Then they ran back to their school.

A man in threadbare, faded working clothes opened the door. He was unshaven and looked at me with suspicion. I apologized for disturbing him. The children brought me to the wrong house. Could he possibly help me? I was looking for a Jesuit priest, *Padre* X. He took my hand in both of his and his face lit up with joy. "Pedro is not home but please come in. This house is yours." The inside was as poor as the outside had led me to expect. He removed stacks of unfolded clothes from a kitchen chair for me to sit. Hastily he cleaned up dirty dishes left on the table. "The five of us live here together," he explained. "Paco will be with us only a short while longer. He is going to Peru to work there among the poor. Pedro works as a day laborer in the sugarcane fields, and Jorge works as a truck driver for the city garbage collection. Jaime and I still study to be priests." I could not have been more unprepared for what I found. "Because I don't work on the outside and earn money, I contribute by cooking for the others. They also partly pay for my studies." Aside from the immediate surroundings, it smacked more of the spirit of the kibbutz than anything else. If these were priests, they were certainly different from all the others I had seen in Spain. Pedro was at the *Cartuja*, and if I wanted to see him I better go there right away. He indicated the way with elaborate details: "Anywhere you ask, everybody in Granada knows the *Cartuja*." This was becoming an almost ritual phrase, but I had reason to doubt its efficacy.

From earlier reading about Granada, I remembered that the *Churriguesque* (Baroque) sacristy of the Carthusian Monastery was described as the Christian counterpart of the Alhambra.

It was about an hour's walk, much of it in open country, which, after the incredible slums, was a relief. Whenever I inquired along the way, people answered me in hushed, reverent tones. The monastery stood on a wooded hill dominating the peaceful surroundings. I inquired at the forbidding main gate after *Padre* X. Having seen where he lived in the shack with the leaky roof and having spoken to one of his companions, I had come to think of him simply as Pedro. I waited for a long time on the steps outside the massive iron grille. I watched the flow of ecclesiastical dignitaries and grew uneasy remembering the *baracones del frigorifico*.

A gaunt, handsome man wearing blue jeans, a red shirt, a sports cap, and green socks came up to me. His tanned face, calloused hands, dusty shoes, and unpriestly attire made him look more like a horsedealer. "I am Pedro," he said. "You asked after me." Startled, I asked him if he was *Padre* X. He winced and repeated, "My name is Pedro. Will you please omit the *Padre*? I don't especially like it." I told him my name was Juan and thus in formal Spain we were on first name basis from the moment we met.

I tried in a few words to tell him who I was. Intrigued by my having grown up with the Gypsies and having published several books about them, he said he had a busy schedule here at the monastery but would I please join him and his companions for dinner that night "at the house."

That night I went back to the *baracones*. We shook hands and Pedro introduced me to the three other companions I had not yet met, and who shared the shack with him. They all wore working clothes. Two of their neighbors, *Gitanos*, were visiting. "These comrades and I work together in the fields. That one over there," he pointed out one of the worker-priests, "until today drove a truck for the *basura*, the garbage disposal. Now he is unemployed. He was fired from his job today."

The atmosphere was open and frank, without reticence and uncomplicated. I was surprised to be so easily included in family affairs and I was appreciative of the easy companionship. In my presence the two *Gitanos* and Pedro talked at length about work conditions and friction with their employer. "The brother of that one," Pedro pointed out one of the *Gitanos*, "was crippled two years ago by the *Guardia Civil* for taking part in a strike. Several workers were shot to death. He was lucky, but now he has trouble getting work. They know he is a trouble-maker." A proud grin spread over his face when he said it, and he put his arm around the Gypsy's shoulders with affection. He added, "Here we are all trouble-makers, all of us." Serious again, he went on, "It is easier for us priests; after all, we have no wives and children to feed." The ex-garbage collector added, "As a priest, that is privileged, I wanted to learn to feel what it is to be a poor laborer. Now, maybe, I will learn what it is to be an unemployed laborer."

Throughout the evening the conversation was about labor conditions, the exploitation of the workers, the abusive treatment of the employer's overseer and police harassment. "Though as priests, and they know we are priests, and Spain is a Catholic country, we are still better treated than the average workers, even though we resent this. We have lived here in the *baracones* over two years. At first the neighbors thought we were police spies making up lists of opposition elements and socialists. During the Civil War we had massacres here, as you know. No wonder people were distrustful. Then they found out we were Jesuit priests, and for a while that did not help either. Now they have grown used to us—as neighbors." We shared the meal prepared by the seminarian and I have to admit that, for men working the fields, it was a humble meal.

From one of the nearby shacks came a loud, wild lament. "That is Perico getting drunk again to get over his despair, while his children try to sleep away their hunger," one of them commented matter-of-factly.

Pedro took me out into the dark alley for a walk through the *barrio* while the others went on discussing gripes and tactics. "All this must bore you," he said outside, "but to us this is our life. Things are not good. It is true they were worse a few years ago but that is no satisfaction for today's hunger."

All doors were closed and windows covered up. We walked in the dark, stumbling on garbage. Through the thin walls of the shacks we could hear every word that was said inside, and it gave me a queasy feeling of gross indiscretion. I felt like an involuntary eavesdropper. I learned that privacy also was a privilege of the well-to-do. In the night somebody rushed by on her way to the public latrines. "That's Fernando's wife. She has a lot of trouble with her plumbing, poor thing."

The *baracones* had originally extended much further but, as the authorities made spaces available elsewhere, shacks here were destroyed. "Tomorrow at dawn I have to go to work, but the day after I will manage to make myself free. Then we can go to visit *Gitanos* in other neighborhoods. Until 1963 many *Gitanos* lived in the caves of the Sacromonte, perhaps as many as ten thousand of them. That year some caves collapsed as a few have collapsed for centuries. The *Guardia Civil* evacuated the entire Sacromonte, forcibly, that goes without saying, and scattered the Gypsies in small groups, some to much better, others to much worse, quarters. They were much easier to control this way. We will go to Virgencica and Zaidin, to Chinaral, to Haza Grande. And remind me to take you to the Baranca del

Beiro. But this is a different story. It is a place where the Gypsies went to live in 1957 of their own free will. As the name indicates, it is in a ravine some sixty feet below the level of the road where many cars pass every day. Few people realize Gypsies live there. It is near the factory of explosives and the water that flows in the ravine is undrinkable. They are very, very poor but independent." Then with what sounded like regret he added, "Any day now we, too, will be forced to evacuate here, from the *baracones del frigorifico.*"

My eyes were adjusted to the darkness and I looked around me and sensed with Pedro how easily, under specific conditions, man can become attached and make himself "at home." It was clear that it was not the roof under which he lived but the people among whom he had become used to live, and I was sure, in Pedro's case, he had come to love.

After dark, more so than at any other time, the *baracones* became the exclusive territory of its inhabitants, providing them with a privacy of sorts.

In his group Pedro was the only one involved with Gypsies. The others each had their own interest in specific social problems. "Throughout Spain there are many others like us," he said, not in answer to a question of mine but as if to reassure himself. "Many of us work individually. A fraction of the Catholic Church here in Spain starts being concerned with social enlightenment. *Caritas* is interested in the problems of the Gypsies. They have their headquarters in Barcelona. You ought to go there and meet them. I know all the people there and will give you introductions. If you care." In fact, I was at that point more interested in getting to know the *Cale* themselves rather than *payo* organizations, however well-intentioned; and in the case of *Caritas* it seemed obvious that they must after all be equally interested in conversion and adherence to Catholicism. After a silence Pedro added, reading my thoughts, "Anyway, I, too, prefer to work alone. I feel closer to the Gypsies than I feel to them." Somewhat later again he mused, "They are often more hindrance than help. They fail to understand why I want to live like a Gypsy and they reproach me for not proselytizing. I think it is more important for me, for us, to understand, to know, to feel what life is about, than to attempt to convert. In the traditional Church we have become too removed from suffering, the daily suffering, the daily struggle against adversity. As priests, we have become righteous instead of practicing that form of obedience to God which is rebellion against unjust authority on earth. We have conveniently forgotten man's preoccupation with getting enough to eat and in winter to keep warm, to procreate and raise his young. As priests we are unfamiliar with police oppression."

He went on talking in the dark, and I listened as we walked back and forth. The tone of his monologue was becoming too confessional, and I wondered where it would lead.

From a shack down one of the alleys came the flat, scratchy sound of a popular Flamenco song, on a *gramophone* record played too loudly. "That is *la Malena*. When she plays these songs it means she is in one of those moods. Let's go!" Pedro's mood and train of thought had changed as abruptly as the Flamenco music had started up.

The hut we entered was the same as that of Pedro and the *curas,* but whereas they slept on hard narrow cots and one double-decker bunk bed, *la Malena*'s shack was half filled by a bed of disproportionate dimensions. The remaining space was nearly filled by a copper *brasero* (charcoal burner) on the floor and Gypsies sitting around it on heaps of rags and dirty clothes. The walls were covered by cheap reproductions of various popular Virgins. That of the *Macarena* was in the place of honor next to several faded family photographs and large paper flowers in bright, acid colors.

La Malena offered Pedro and me *Quitapenas,* warm wine with cinnamon, sugar, and spices. *Quitapenas* in Spanish means "remover of sorrows." She pushed back the tangled bedcovers and, insisting I would be more comfortable there than on the floor, made me sit there. Pedro's friend, *mi paisano,* fellow countryman, he had called me, should be treated as the best. Pedro beamed and he too joined me on the bed. To make

more space on the floor, the hand-cranked phonograph was also put on the bed, but it would not function properly. A young man joined us on the bed and held the phonograph upright and in proper balance on his lap. The speed was uneven, the volume was overly loud, shattering the sounds, distorting the words.

The room had an animal muskiness and it was very hot. The people who had sat on the floor scrambled to their feet and stood flattening themselves against the wall and door. I could not determine *la Malena*'s age. She lived with her mother and she had a son twelve or thirteen years of age. He was a gaunt, handsome boy, intelligent-looking but precociously tempered by shrewd ghetto sensibilities. She had the kind of ugliness which, instead of repelling, attracted. I knew how Gypsy women in the slums matured precociously and wilted early. Pedro appreciatively described her to me as a *salero,* a salt shaker. She was talkative and had a mocking, tumultuous wit and devilish sort of gaiety.

First the boy danced; but too impatient to hold herself back, she pushed him aside in mock competition. She could dance, but in her attempt at humor she caricatured Flamenco dancing to the point of sheer grotesqueness. Her guests, Pedro included, were apoplectic with laughter. She flared her nostrils and undid her hair. "*¡Viva la Chunga! ¡Viva la Chunga!*" they all roared. They apparently knew her special imitation number of the well-known dancer by that name. She breathed heavily. She hitched up her short, narrow skirt, hips eddying. I could see how such raw animal passion could offend the more austere Iberian temperament.

Pedro and I went together one day to the Barrio de la Virgencica. It was in a new section, in a semi-rural setting, on the outskirts of Granada. It had been built after a prize-winning architect's plans, brilliantly conceived but shoddily executed. Four dwellings, back to back, in a star formation, shared one single high roof sloping down from a conelike middle. The variations of height of ceilings, from perhaps twelve feet to eight feet, six inches, gave the interior character and a potential for individual improvisation.

Each apartment had an entrance facing a different direction, adding a sense of privacy. The roads between them were concrete. Trees had been planted, a rare consideration in Spain, and allowance had been made for extensive flower beds and low shrubs. On the other hand, there seemed to be no adequate garbage disposal facilities.

Angelito had recently come to La Virgencica and he seemed happy about the change. He lived on the far side of the colony at the edge of the fields. When we arrived, he was working in his forge, beating the red hot iron and singing lustily. A number of Gypsy blacksmiths lived here in the new village, but they were not sure yet of their status: Could they, yes or no, practice their trade here? They were therefore careful not to work at late hours that might disturb their non-Gypsy neighbors, and they watched that the smoke from their forges did not inconvenience them too much, at least for now. Angelito explained that living on the very outskirts made all this easier and he used an expression in *Calo* that escaped me but that I interpreted to mean he had used some kind of bribery to obtain this advantage.

"The *Guardia Civil* keeps a strict control on who comes and goes," he said, somewhat surprised that we had not been intercepted. "Several cousins of mine who came to visit me were turned away by them because they could not prove they lived here. Now they come at night through the fields."

We had wine and olives stuffed with anchovies, but a child kept the bellows working and the forge fire roaring. Soon Angelito went back to hammering the red hot iron into shape. He worked in short bursts, continued the conversation, worked again, and sang in between. He earned his living by making small wrought iron objects, the *cosas tipicas* sold to tourists through fellow Gypsy intermediaries. For purely Spanish consumption he made the special nails with heavy stud-heads still much in use in the South to ornament outside doors; but above all he liked to make *rejas,* wrought iron window grilles. In these he could match his imagination with his technical skills. With the pride of the artist, he showed us how out of a piece of iron he could shape a rose, a vine leaf with spiral tendrils, or a branch with thorns. Inside the house he showed us a variety of small objects and toys he had made for his children and for his wife: a wrought iron doll's chair and miniature bed, a small guitar and flat Andalusian hat, fantastic doorknobs, and even a crucifix.

After dark, many other Gypsies, relatives and friends of Angelito's, came to the house. The conversation was lively and interesting. Angelito and another blacksmith sang *tonas de la fragua,* songs of the forge, tapping scraps of iron in the slow, steady cadence of the hammer on the anvil by way of accompaniment.

On another day we went to the colony of Zaidin. It was overpopulated and looked rough. Rows of mean, low wooden buildings were closely set together. We were assailed by hordes of rowdy, disheveled Gypsy children. When Pedro told them whom we were visiting, their attitude changed from openly aggressive to just plain bothersome; and they followed us to make sure we were who we had said we were and we went to visit those we said we would. If not. . . .

In spite of the heat, most people living in the Zaidin sat outside in the narrow passageways rather than inside where it was cooler. It was with difficulty that we found the Gypsy family Pedro was looking for. Pedro apparently had not been here for a while, the rows of shacks all looked alike, and the children were not much help. When we eventually found them, Pedro was warmly greeted and received as a long lost relative. The head of the family was a stout man with a loud, violent manner. He embraced Pedro and addressed him with the familiar and endearing diminutive of Pedro, *Perico.* It was a large family and, after their father, they looked like a wild bunch.

Two dilapidated chairs were brought from inside the house for us to sit on. They themselves crouched or sat on the dirt floor. In spite of our protests, the children were reprimanded for crowding too close to us. A cranky looking old woman, *la abuela de nosotros todos,* the grandmother of all of us, they called her, nearly pulled Pedro from his chair. She snatched the chair from under him and violently threw it aside. Pedro laughed, but at first nobody seemed to know quite what to make of it. I was unsure what to do in case I were next to draw her attention. Scowling, she said, without addressing anybody in particular, "How dare you make *el Padre Potaje,* the reverend father Soup [I later learned this was one of the various nicknames the Gypsies had given him, this particular one to celebrate his liking for soup] sit down on that chair!" By now they all burst out in merry laughter at a private joke we were not in on. The *abuela de nosotros todos* then addressed us directly: "Why do you think everybody here in Zaidin is sitting outside in the sun? Why do you think? Because those of the Zaidin have gone crazy?" Now it was the turn of all the members of the family to try to hush her up, but they couldn't. "Because these wooden houses and all the furniture inside of them are crawling with *chinches,* bedbugs, that's why! I don't want them to eat up alive our beloved *Padre Potaje.*" Now that the truth was known, they started laughing again, though some of them said *"¡que lachi!"* what a shame on us!

The doors of many shanties were nailed shut. They explained to us that many of the people living here had gone back on the road and stayed there for months at a time. They kept the house as their official residence only for the sake of their legal status. These Gypsies lived off the land as well as they could but tried to avoid the onerous label of nomads. The doors of the houses had no locks; therefore it had become the custom to simply nail shut the doors—*pro tem.*

On the way home we passed a group of *Gitanos* gesticulating wildly. They shouted hoarsely. The women sniveled and cried, their hair disheveled. They had come from a *velatorio,* a funeral wake.

On another occasion, Pedro took me to meet what he described, using the French term, as Gypsy bourgeoisie. The house they lived in was solid middle-class and it was furnished in uninspiringly dull but "proper" midthirties clutter. They received us courteously but with a certain reserve. I realized this could be due to Pedro's image, in their context, as a radical. They received him because, after all, he was a Jesuit priest, but

they were leery of his unorthodox interest in all those unassimilated, no-good outcasts. They themselves had been able to adjust. They were good Catholics. After all, they worked at steady jobs. They saved up money and invested in property. So why didn't these others—Gypsies, because after all that was what they were—do the same?

At the house we were introduced to the *caballeros de Cordoba,* the gentlemen from Cordoba. They owned and ran a shoe factory in that city. If it had not been for Pedro's keen sense of observation, and a rare show of "obnoxious activism" on his part, I would never have guessed they were Gypsies too. There was a vague something not entirely Iberian about them, but nothing more serious than could have been explained away or passed on from a Jewish or Moorish ancestor in the distant past, like so many people have in Spain. But *Gitano? Ni pensar,* hardly.

We soon left and, once outside, Pedro triumphantly said, "Now you have seen them all, from the poorest, most rejected to the . . . ." He did not finish his sentence.

Soon afterward, Pedro took the overnight bus to Barcelona, traveling some twenty-seven hours nonstop. He had told me one day he had a brother who lived there whose daughter was celebrating her First Communion. He would very much have liked to go and, from Barcelona, go on to the Gypsy pilgrimage at the Saintes-Maries-de-la-Mer, in the Camargue, not far from Arles, in France, but . . . *"Ni hablar.* There is nothing to talk about. I consider it a privilege to have you as my guest, and that is that." I had planned to go for a few days to Madrid, during which time he could attend to family obligations, and I would join him in Barcelona. After that we would go together to the Saintes-Maries, where I had never been.

When I lived with the *Rom* in the nineteen thirties and forties, they had never even heard of the pilgrimage to Saintes-Maries. It was in 1960 that for the first time a *Rom* I knew in Paris mentioned it, planning to attend. He had explained to me that since all those tourists went there to see the Gypsies, it might be a good idea for him to go there to see the tourists. Somewhat redundantly he had added, "to do business."

On their way, Gypsies stop for a time in the city, and gauge its capacity to yield something for them. They dwell on the outskirts, not in slums but in resting places. In the permanent, possession-ridden city, the Gypsies are intrusive visitors. They hawk flowers and nonsense, bootblack and beg. The begging women project a wretched, impoverished facade, but every coin gotten is proof of their skill, and they answer the gift with unspoken, contemptuous curses.

The more determined
nomads set up
ramshackle lean-tos;
those playing the role
of more permanent
dwellers erect an
unlocked tent of stone
or mortar, provided
only with the barest
necessities, for
possessions stifle and
kill.

*They abhor the values of
the settled community
—their permanence is
their inner freedom.*

Clean as a Sunday Madrileño, but underneath, lice are a hearty lot.

Chapter 9
In Madrid

Evaluated Gypsies in Madrid. And more slums in Barcelona.

IN Madrid I met several young intellectuals interested in the problem of the Gypsies. One was the anthropologist Juan Aguirre, the other the promising architect and urbanist Pablo Carvajal. They were enthusiastic, eager, and very generous. With and through them I met a large number of Gypsies. We visited the popular neighborhoods of La Celsa, Fuencarral, Lara, Lucero, Altamira, La China, and Puente de Vallecas. They also took me to visit a well-organized cooperative furniture factory run by Gypsies. The discussion there was almost exclusively about the lack of jobs and opportunity. They felt the present government had lagged in industrial development and feared their country would become to the European community a mere source of cheap manpower, a stockpile of raw materials, and an inexpensive vacation ground for the more affluent masses from the neighboring countries. Listening to them, I almost forgot they were Gypsies.

They spoke slyly about "those from Barcelona" who were only interested in participating in international congresses and who wanted to promote a new, synthetic, common Gypsy language "for all the Gypsies of the whole world." "The *Hungaros* have their own language," they said, "and it makes their strength. We have lost ours. What would it help if we now started to learn it all over? To listen to them talk about the Gypsies' new identity and shallow utopia of an independent Gypsy nation, you would think they are more *payo* than we *apayados*! What we need are jobs, integration, and some degree of social justice instead of all that romantic *payo* hodge-podge."

As we had agreed before we separated, I picked up Pedro at his elder brother's toy shop in Barcelona. After we had lunch together, Pedro insisted on showing me the city where he grew up. Though my primary interest was in seeing Gypsies, he took me to see Gaudi's Sagrada Familia, Tibidao, Montjuich, and the Roman excavations beneath the cathedral, La Seu. He showed me the church where he was baptized and the slum neighborhood where he celebrated his first mass. He took me to the Ramblas and made a point for me to see the Sardana being danced at the Plaza Cataluña. As a concession, and a reprieve from indoctrinating me in his, until now unsuspected, Catalan particularism, he took me to a record shop where we went on a wild buying spree of Flamenco and *Cante Hondo* records. Barcelona was a prosperous, bourgeois city of over two million inhabitants. The Catalans were hardworking and progressive—I did not dispute any of the things Pedro wanted to tell me about them, but I had Gypsies on my mind, and our time here was short.

We duly went to the offices of *Caritas*, the Catholic charity organization, met and talked to all the good people in charge of various valid social and religious programs. We listened to Juan de Dios Ramirez Heredia, editor of *Pomezia*, expound about the Gypsy World Congress of April 1971, in London, which he had just attended. They could not have been more helpful. However, I soon found out they were more interested in the "good" Gypsies while, unaccountably, from their point of view, by temperament, I was more inclined toward the "bad" ones.

At the approaches of Montjuich we found a few hovels, worse perhaps than I had seen elsewhere, where some of the Amayas lived, relatives of the late and much admired dancer of international fame, Carmen. They received Pedro with clamors of joy; and it was good to see what contact with the Gypsies did to Pedro. If he knew it or not, here he was in his element. Showing me the sights and visiting with his brothers, Pedro had shown me a side of his I was alien to, even incompatible with.

Pedro had been close to the Amaya family since the days he still studied for the priesthood and lived in Barcelona. In spite of their apparent poverty, they seemed to be a happy lot, and there was much joking and lightheartedness. I had seen Carmen Amaya and her troupe dance in London, New York, and elsewhere; it was hard to reconcile the clamor and glamor she had been surrounded with and the present state in which these other Amayas lived today. One of the Amaya girls had many years ago married a French commercial photographer who worked in Barcelona, and with whom we spent a pleasant and informative evening. He was leaving the following day at dawn for the Saintes-Maries-de-la-Mer with his wife and their grown children. We made arrangements to meet there.

We crossed the railroad tracks into a vast no man's land covered by widely scattered shanties of all kinds and varieties. It was possibly the largest such settlement I had seen in Spain. The blue Mediterranean in the background, the clear, pungent smell of the sea and soft swish of the waves, made it look like a resort. In the center stood *el castillo*, a central administrative building and settlement school, built like a small-scale castle, hence its name. It had a large court, used as a school yard, surrounded by high cement-covered walls, into which, when it was still wet, the children had been encouraged to scratch their own highly-effective designs. Next to the school, the settlement ran a *co-operativa* where paper flowers were made; pincushions, potholders, and aprons sewn for sale on the outside. There was a household school and a building trade school for boys.

Now that he was again among Gypsies, Pedro wanted to visit a priest he knew and had not seen in many years, who lived in the Gypsy settlement of the Campo de la Bota, at the edge of the sea. Most Gypsy neighborhoods had been "cleaned up" by the authorities in recent years.

Away from the center, the rows of shan-ties were more rundown, garbage more visible. Beyond this zone lay the outer fringe of miserable lean-tos, broken-down carts, and improvised tents of the semi-nomads. Large fires burned on the beach, and here we ran into a group of wild-looking Gypsies in incredible rags. They were a mixture of *canasteros,* basket makers and animal traders. They hailed us, with an edge of defiance, perhaps even an implied menace. They jestingly invited us to join them by their fires, which we did. They were on their own territory and the stretch we had gotten lost in was deserted. Neither Pedro nor I showed signs of being ill at ease. They changed their tactics and invited us to share their meal of sardines roasted over the open fire. With them we shared *pipas,* roasted sunflower seeds, demonstratively spitting out the shells, which opened the way to an unexpected evening of humorous banter and repartee, of fun and mimicry, like an entertaining bargaining for a horse.

In the distance, we could hear and see the noises and lights of the big city and, on the opposite side, the unlit sky over the sea and the lapping of the waves on the Mediterranean beach. We left at dawn. Many of the women and children were asleep, and the men had exhausted whatever hostility against outsiders they might have felt earlier in the evening. We walked back along the beach before turning inland and back to the city. Sleepy and at peace, totally unsuspecting, we walked into what, too late, shocked me back to my senses. I knew it was an ambush. Cold and hard I felt the gun pressed into my back, at rib-height. It was only the *Guardia Civil,* whose duty they felt it was to check our identity and find the explanation for the late outing. As a rule, the police in Spain were polite to foreigners.

In "wartime" the Campo de la Bota area had been used for mass executions, where thousands died at the *paredon,* against the wall, pockmarked by bullets where victims were shot. "They executed many people," Pedro said, without specifying which of the antagonists in the Spanish Civil War he referred to, or maybe to him this was obvious, "but then the other side killed as many."

121

Chapter 10
Division

Pilgrimage to the
Saintes-Maries-de-la-Mer
in France. The Gypsies
and the outsiders,
and unexpected
division between Gypsies
and Gypsies.

BEFORE going to the Camargue, it occurred to me to invite along for the trip, Karen, a young friend of mine of the flower generation and drug subculture, now living with her photographer boyfriend in the Balearic Islands. I flew to Ibiza, and they seemed delighted with the idea and contributed to the expedition the use of their Volkswagen pick-up truck.

Often in the past, when I spoke about Gypsies, I found people sought to make association between the Gypsies and the life style of the "hippies" and members of the communes. My reaction to this, independent from where my sympathies lay, was that the obvious differences far superseded the possible and superficial similarities.

Karen and Hunter came to Barcelona with their truck by the overnight ferry, and the same day we drove over the Pyrenees to the swamps of the Camargue. It had rained heavily, and roads were flooded. In the middle of the night we arrived at the Saintes-Maries-de-la-Mer, over which brooded the beautiful eleventh-century fortress-church.

Thousands of trailers, caravans, and trucks adapted into mobile homes were parked on both sides of every street of the village and even along the beach. It was strangely exhilarating to see that many nomads, albeit motorized, assembled in one place. At night the village itself looked deserted, but everywhere, between the trailers and around camp-

fires, groups of wanderers were celebrating. We drove around looking for an open spot. Several times we circled the entire area before we found a place on the far end of the village.

We woke up to a general and noisy commotion of thousands of newly-arrived campers waking up, hustling for water, rushing to the local shops for bread, milk, eggs, and meat while the supplies lasted. Walking around, we were surprised to see so few Gypsies. The majority were French-speaking and of French extraction, leading a nomadic Gypsy-like existence. We went to the church which was, after all, the center of all the activities. Here we found as many tourists as nomads; I could not bring myself to refer to them as Gypsies, which they were not. They called themselves "voyageurs" or travelers.

Then we ran into large groups of hippies in full paraphernalia. They were everywhere "Gypsying"—but not Gypsies. Super-nomads, perhaps, seeking salvation on the roads.

We sat down in the shade of a café terrace watching the world go by. A well-organized squad of solid-looking Gypsy women staked out their hunting territory around the old church and briskly started their saturation operation—fortune-telling, selling blessed medals, begging, posing for photographers, for a price, or just plain intimidating tourists.

Here finally were the true *Rom* I had grown up with, who both repelled and attracted, whom I could converse with in their own language, and felt at home with in spite of everything which apparently should have separated us.

They wore brightly-colored, long, full skirts, their long black hair in braids under the *diklo*, the kerchief. They wore an outrageous amount of solid gold pieces, gold bracelets, earrings and pendants—all while begging. I spoke to them, and to Pedro's visible joy, we were invited, wined and dined and entertained. There I met Madel, an impressive looking woman of about sixty, who was the daughter of Notarka, a woman whom I had known in Spain toward the end of the Second World War. In 1966 I had met one of her cousins, Borinka in Peru and later in Mexico. I also knew her brother Pepe who was now in Australia. They drove the latest model Mercedes-Benz and American cars. They apologized for not throwing a more extensive welcoming party for me, one of their traditional *patshiva,* but coming here to the pilgrimage of the Saintes-Maries-de-la-Mer was, as I must understand, strictly business.

We sat at our favorite café terrace and waited there till the people we wanted to meet passed by. Pedro introduced me to the French Abbé Barthélémy, to Père Fleury, to Don Bruno Nicolini of Rome, and the sociologist Mirella Karpati, editor of *Lacio Drom*. I knew them by name from my reading and they knew of me, but we had not met before.

A large group of *Sinti* musicians played for the tourists at various café terraces. Again I ran into people I had known twenty-five years ago, relatives of my good friend Hoyok Mehrstein of the popular Schuckenak Quartet and relatives of the late jazz guitarist Django Reinhardt.

Several TV crews, one Japanese, were bustling about. There were reporters and impresarios, and deals were being made; and there was the highly promoted, de rigueur, supposedly "incognito" appearance of Manita de Plata, the French-based virtuoso Flamenco guitarist sneered at by the Spanish. And there was an "exclusive" performance by the contender Jose Pisa inside the barricaded church.

Somehow the atmosphere felt tense. The sharp division between the local inhabitants and the strangers became painfully evident; next, friction flared up between tourists and their Gypsy harassers, between the hippies and the tourists, between the French police and the hippies, between the Gypsies and the hippies, between the *Rom* and the *Sinti*. And finally between the Spanish *Gitanos* living in France and those few who had come from Spain. To me the pilgrimage of the Saintes-Maries-de-la-Mer painfully divided people, even when, often, they made do and tried hard to put up with each other for a few days.

After the wake at the crypt of Sainte Sara and the procession in which she was taken to the sea, all the Gypsies departed hurriedly; business, cynically, had been taken care of for another year; many of the other nomads followed suit. A controversy raged about the statute of canonization of Sainte Sara; therefore her procession took place one day "to satisfy the Gypsies" and that of the true Saints, the Saintes Maries, honored by the locals, on the following day.

Under a gray sky, threatening more rain, the exodus started.

We hurried back to Sevilla to be there in time for that other pilgrimage we had made a vow to attend: the *romeria de la Virgen del Rocio*.

Chapter 11
Celebration

Romeria del Rocio, gay pilgrimage-picnic to the shrine of the Virgin of the Dew in the swamplands of the Guadalquivir estuary. Flamenco singing and dancing in a mad overflow of emotion.

WE were once again in Sevilla. Throughout the trip back Pedro had been saying he hoped to convince his friend Rafael and some of the other *Gitanos* to join us on the pilgrimage of El Rocio. As the days went by, Pedro had become more enthusiastic about the prospect. For a while I had unresolved feelings but was nonetheless easily swayed, enjoying his friendship and looking forward to meeting those he referred to as his *Gitano* family. At first I was torn by a vague, perhaps ambiguous, sense of family obligation to accompany on the *romeria del Rocio* the members of the brotherhood from the ancestral village of Corria del Rio. Somewhat predictably, Pedro and the *Cale* won out.

It was noon and we hung around idly between the Barrio de Santa Cruz and the cathedral "hoping to find Rafael," as Pedro had put it without further precision about time or place.

At this time of the day, tourist guides, almond venders, peddlers of *cosas tipicas*, souvenirs, miniature copper wares and wrought iron, gathered near the Plaza de los Reyes. Pedro knew many of them; and to my surprise I discovered that many of them were *Gitanos*.

Someone invited us for a drink at the nearby Alcasar Bar. "Rafael's cousin," Pedro whispered to me, I suspected, to entice me. Other *Gitanos* joined us. This appeared to be their usual hangout. We drank coffee and brandy. The conversations were very animated and exclusively about business and the tourist trade. It reminded me of a combination horsemarket, auction sale, and racetrack meet. Pedro, who was in his element and enjoying every moment of it, inquired after people they knew in common. At the time of the *Feria,* which now seemed long ago, I had stayed around the corner, just a few doors away, in a part of the world that had nothing in common with the present one.

At lunch time suddenly everybody left. Pedro put his arm through mine and took me outside. "Rafael expects us to have lunch with him at home," he said casually, and there, waiting for us on the sidewalk, was one of the many *Gitanos* I had shaken hands with, never expecting him to be the Rafael I had heard so much about. The meeting was most undramatic. This was typical Gypsy casualness. After the trip together to the Saintes-Maries-de-la-Mer, and the discovery of Pedro's Catalan birth and upbringing in middle-class Barcelona I had forgotten what he was capable of. As proudly a Catalan as he had proved to be in the North, as nonchalant an Andalus he was once again among the *Gitanos* of southern Spain.

On the way, Rafael kept meeting people he knew and wanted to talk to. Most of them were *Gitanos,* assimilated into Spanish everyday life to the extent of being hardly identifiable as *Gitanos* to outsiders. Every hundred feet or so we slowed down or stopped while Rafael embraced one more acquaintance or relative, or walked away with him in a direction opposite to ours for a conspiratorial aside. The overly casual manner and his lack of consideration began to irritate me. In his appearance or behavior he was a far cry from the affectionate descriptions Pedro had given me of him. I thought he looked an *apayado,* Hispanized, petty hustler or an itinerant peddler. There was nothing distinctive about any of his features. Nothing about him stood out. He was of average height. He wore a tweed sport jacket, dark trousers, and highly polished, yellow shoes. I wondered what Pedro, whose judgment I had come to trust, could possibly have seen in this shallow, indifferent little man, who called up in me echoes of seedy rooming houses and cheap transient hotels....

Rafael lived on a quiet side street, off a main artery, in a rather affluent quarter on the outskirts of Sevilla. There were ten houses on either side of the street "all inhabited by us, *Gitanos*." We were surrounded by a swarm of well-fed, well-dressed, and well-behaved, beaming Gypsy children. Several of them threw themselves at Pedro and hung affectionately from his neck and shoulders. Others jumped onto Pedro, hugging him. We were ushered inside. The house was spacious and clean. From everywhere, relatives and friends came to welcome us. Rafael had many children, several handsome teenage sons and several shy, pretty daughters, the youngest of whom was about six or seven. Rafael's wife had died a few years ago. When I came inside the house, her photograph, next to the image of the *Virgen de la Macarena*, was the first thing that had been pointed out to me. Rafael offered us *cañas* of Manzanilla wine. *Cañas* are the special narrow, tall glasses in which sherry was traditionally served.

Our arrival had created a subdued commotion. Pedro said, "In Rafael's and in my own name this is your house. Until now you were a friend, to be helped and served, now you are as good as a relative. It is up to you to make yourself at home as well as you can." To emphasize Pedro's words, Rafael asked me to bring him another bottle of Jerez "from the kitchen." He added in a bantering tone, "That should truly teach you to be a relative!"

It was a revelation to see the extent to which Pedro functioned better here and was more at ease than he had been at the homes of his own brothers in Catalonia.

Rafael exchanged the sports cap he wore to work for the tourists and put on his own *Gitano* cap. He took off the 35mm single-reflex camera that hung around his neck and handed it for safekeeping to one of his sons "until we come back from El Rocio." This was the first inkling I got of the fact that he had decided to join Pedro and me, and, in Gypsy fashion, it was tossed off *en passant*.

We were joined by Rafael's father. He proudly told me that all his sons had become, after him, great photographers. Tourist photographers, he specified. He himself had started many years ago, "when photography had just been invented," to make portraits at country fairs. I had been fascinated by the anachronistic survival throughout rural Spain of this kind of photographers with their props of a large toy fighting bull or a fiercely rearing imitation horse to pose with or on. The backgrounds, too, were often quaintly charming: a Moorish castle or even the *Giralda* painted on a backdrop. "Now my sons photograph foreigners from all the nations on earth, right in front of the *Giralda*, mind you." Passing through darkened bedrooms, he took me to the patio full of blooming geraniums and showed me the darkroom.

We had a lavish meal, to which, as I later found out, all the neighbors had contributed to do Rafael and Pedro proud. The two of them acted like brothers, and they were constantly referred to as co-hosts. When Rafael's wife had died, Pedro, already an ordained Jesuit priest, had taken over the responsibility for the children and the running of the household for close to two years. The youngest child had still been in diapers. Pedro had lived with them while Rafael worked on the outside to feed his brood. They were a delightfully cooperative and affectionate family. Meeting his children and knowing his relatives gave Rafael a dimension I had not previously suspected.

While Pedro and Rafael went for a long walk to talk undisturbed, the rest of the family took turns entertaining me. I was taken from house to house, up and down the *Gitano* street. The Gypsies were full of questions and wonder about the world I came from, about Pedro and my trip to the Saintes-Maries. Apparently he had already found occasion to whet their curiosity, also with tales about the *Hungaros* we had seen together there and my relationship to them. The day and the evening went by and I enjoyed the family atmosphere. Our leaving in the morning for the Las Marismas swamplands to go to El Rocio was not mentioned again and, as far as I could see, no preparations were made for it.

When I woke up the next morning, well-rested, in a good mood, and raring to go, Pedro and Rafael had already left the house and nobody knew where they went or when they would return. I was anxious to leave and did not relish spending another day, however pleasant in itself, hanging around with noth-

ing to do and not in control of my schedule and activities. I had been away from the Gypsies too long for that. I suddenly remembered a *Rom* saying that it was senseless, and undignified, to rush "as you could, in this manner, only rush to your own death instead of just waiting for it to come to you." Here I was living with a *Gitano* family, free to observe and absorb, and I was feeling restless.

Toward early afternoon, Pedro and Rafael came back in a social, boisterous mood. They looked like accomplices in some rather shady deal. Their eyes had an unnatural shine, and they smelled of wine. They shook me out of my moodiness. "Let's go, let's go," they shouted, "what are we waiting for? On to El Rocio. *Viva la Blanca Paloma,*" which was, as I later learned, the favorite and endlessly repeated cry of the pilgrims to El Rocio. We took off abruptly amidst a commotion of relatives, friends, and neighbors rushing up to wish us Godspeed, and with promises to catch up with us there.

On the road in the heat the enthusiasm subsided, though Rafael kept singing the traditional songs of El Rocio, *rocieros,* banging out the accompaniment on the guitar instead of playing it. He shouted loudly to people along the road, asking them if this was the right way to go to El Rocio, to which, with shouts almost equal to his, or as exaggerated, they replied that it was the right road. Every few minutes he interrupted his singing long enough to ask the same question. It seemed obsessive and needless until I realized that this was part of the ritual, informing everybody that we were on our way to the pilgrimage and asking for acknowledgment. "Is this the right way to El Rocio?" became simply a refrain, which in time I, too, started repeating. The closer we came to El Rocio, the more boisterous became both question and answer. Most of the time there was only one road obviously going to one destination. The road to El Rocio was, so to speak, a dead-end road leading nowhere else. The pretense of asking was part of the holiday mood, like being in a race and drawing strength and endurance from fans cheering one on.

We passed other caravans of exuberantly decorated carts perched high on two outsized wheels and with a sheltering canvas cover.

Horsemen wove their way in and out between them, preceding and following them. Cheering and laughter was universal.

At the approaches to each village or hamlet, women and children lined the road to see the pilgrims pass. They offered fruit or snacks and passed around the water-*poron* or wine-skin. Rafael kept on meeting people he knew, and the entire trek resembled one joyous family reunion. The sun was hot and the amount of wine we consumed extravagant.

We stopped at a village where Rafael had some friends. We walked around the butchers' stalls at the open-air market. Dogs were gnawing on large bones. The display of meats was gory, to say the least. Rafael ordered kilos of freshly made blood sausage and kilos of *chorizo* and kilos of cured ham. My offer to pay for it was vehemently rejected. Rafael asked how much it amounted to. Bantering back and forth, the butcher asked him where we were going. When Rafael melodramatically answered to El Rocio the butcher extended both hands, shaking them in a gesture of negation, and replied that from pilgrims he could not accept money. Rafael in turn protested that neither could he order a substantial amount of meat and not pay for it. That he could not accept. "In that case allow me the privilege of being your guest and sharing your food tomorrow at El Rocio," was the answer. It was received with cheers and loud *"Viva la Virgen del Rocio,"* which sounded as a war cry. They embraced in the fashion of Andalusia, clapping each other on the back. Pedro and I were embraced in turn and the generous butcher clapped us on the back, and we, him.

Next we stopped at a small village called Benacasón. The heat shimmered over the plain and the blazing sunlight refracted blindingly from the squat whitewashed houses.

One of Rafael's friends this time was not a *Gitano*, but a pure Andalus and the owner of a wine cellar. Proudly, he took us inside the huge shed filled with casks of the local pale, sourish, dry wine. With a brisk, expert gesture, he plunged a long wooden rod with a scoop at the end into a cask and took out the amount of a *caña* for us to sample. We sampled dark, golden sherry, medium dry and of great body; others light, more delicate, topaz in color, with a slight taste of almond; and yet others very

rich and full, or dry and crisp and light. After much tasting and appreciating and discussion, we left without buying anything after all. I had suggested that since Rafael had bought the meat I would be happy to contribute the wine, but Pedro took me aside and firmly informed me this was to be Rafael's party. Period.

Accompanied by the owner of the wine cellar, we went on to the local inn. I wondered why with all that we had already consumed we had to go to one more inn, or why the owner of the wine cellar came with us.

We ate *tapas* and had wine. The most delicious cooked shrimps I ever had anywhere were at the inn in Benacasón. From the innkeeper we got a motley collection of empty bottles—to fill up with the wine Rafael had chosen. The wine cellar sold it only by the cask. The empty bottles were of wide variety: Coca Cola, Cinzano, Burgundy, and Champagne. They had accumulated at the inn over a period of time. At El Rocio, whenever Rafael opened a bottle of Burgundy, Coca Cola, or Cinzano, I had to remember, in anticipation of the taste of its content, not to be misled by the label.

We crossed the wooded, sandy plain toward Almonte, leaving behind the last inhabited shanties and skirting the vast salt marshes infested by reptiles and mosquitoes. Las Marismas came about when erosion choked off the flow of the Guadalquivir and turned the area, once fertile, well-irrigated lands cultivated under the Moors, into a wilderness. On the fringe of it, herds of steers grazed peacefully, until the moment of truth in the ring when they would be butchered. A section of the Las Marismas swamplands, the Coto Doñana, has become a bird sanctuary.

We traveled through vast expanses of wastelands and sand dunes. We arrived at El Rocio in the endless blue twilight of Andalusia. From every direction carts and wagons, drawn by oxen or mules, and a few trucks were arriving. Numerous horsemen crisscrossed the central Plaza Real del Rocio. After parading about to announce the arrival of their contingent, they rode around the shrine to salute the *Virgen del Rocio*; then they went off to look for a spot to set up camp.

There were several streets with sprawling *caravanserai* of sorts that served for the duration of the *romeria* as gathering places and hospitality centers for each brotherhood, or *hermandad*. A few well-to-do Andalusian families also had permanent houses here. During fifty-one weeks out of the year, the village of El Rocio was deserted with only a caretaker to look after the place.

At one side there was a large eucalyptus grove where early arrivals, almost exclusively Gypsies, had already erected their tents. Many fires were lit and burned bright in the oncoming night. The smoke of burning aromatic brushwood mingled with the pungent smell of the salt marshes.

We found an open space and set up camp fairly near the entrance of the village proper "so that when we are ready to leave, we will not be caught in the bottleneck." Water was at a premium and public toilet facilities nonexistent. "Tens of thousands of pilgrims come here every year and they have managed until now. So why should you worry about it this year?"

From early morning on the following day, caravans arrived from every part of Andalusia. I woke up by the shrill squeak of an unoiled hub and the rumbling of many carts. The air throbbed with the wild pounding of hooves of vast cavalcades and the heavy snorts of overheated mule teams. "*¡Viva la Virgen del Rocio!*" shouted those who arrived. "*¡Viva la Blanca Paloma!*" was the answer. Others raised the cry "*¡Viva!*" or "*¡Sin pecado!*"—without sin—"*¡Viva! ¡Viva!*" From this moment on and for the next days, cries of praise to the Virgin were shouted enthusiastically and almost without interruption.

Horses cantered and pranced and milled about, reminiscent of a more egalitarian Sevillan *feria* set in a bucolic setting. I was not aware of any class distinction being made. The drinking here was probably less restrained or decorous. I could see caravans and small advance parties of horsemen from miles away surrounded in a haze of red dust, now spreading, now coalescing. We slowly shook off the night's languor. We went to the entrance of the village to watch the carts and horses arriving. Some came from far away and had been traveling for several days.

Everywhere open-air bars and refreshment stands sprang up. Peddlers set up their booths and stalls. From one of them we bought the special medallike emblem representing the beloved *Virgen del Rocio,* hanging from a long purple, red, or green twisted silk cord. Everyone wore it as the badge of pilgrimhood.

The air was filled with singing of either *rocieros,* songs with lyrics dedicated to this particular Virgin, or *Cante Hondo.* There was uninterrupted and spontaneous dancing.

During the ovenlike noonday heat, activities slackened. Half dazed by heat and wine, we took our *siesta* in the shade underneath the wagon, as did everybody else. Afterwards, accompanied by Pedro and Rafael, I went to the headquarters of the *Hermandad* of Coria del Rio, of which, when I visited the village, I had been made an honorary member. Like that of the *Hermandades* of other localities, the one of my father's village consisted of a sprawling, whitewashed adobe building which housed a large meeting hall, a series of small rooms with beds where members could sleep, a provision room, stables for the riding horses and fodder storage, and a vast kitchen. It had a row of charcoal stoves set into a tiled shelf and a stone sink. These buildings enclosed a large, open quadrangle where the wagons were lined up and the oxen and mules were tied up. There also was a well.

An impressive double-width gate, surmounted by a campanile with a small bronze bell, led to what in fact was a *caravanserai.*

We were gallantly received by Señor José Parra Jimenes who went out of his way to accommodate me. In Coria del Rio they had hoped until their departure that I would arrive in time to join their caravan. A horse was at my disposal and so was a bed anytime I needed a few hours' sleep.

Wine was poured and soon hot food was put on the table for my guests and myself. Señor Parra was a sturdy, heavyset man in his early fifties. In spite of his courteous behavior and his easy going appearance, it was obvious he was used to commanding. He was the *encargado* and at my disposal. While we were there, members of the *Hermandad* presented me their homages in memory of my grandfather, Don Jorge. I overheard Señor Parra explain to someone that Don Jorge had been the *cacique.* From reading about the Mexican Indians, I knew this was some kind of priest-chieftain, but I had never heard the term used in connection with anybody in the homeland. When I asked him, he just smiled a very special smile which told me nothing.

To avoid possible misunderstanding, I had introduced Pedro, perhaps against his pleasure, as a *Padre Jesuita,* hoping his official title would mitigate his appearance. Señor Parra commented to his face that for a priest he certainly was *agitanado.* Again I had never before heard the adjective used. I understood that it meant Gypsified, the opposite of the term *apayado,* like the Spanish or Hispanized, which I kept hearing among the Gypsies. Ever after Señor Parra referred to him as *el Padre Gitano.* I noticed to my distress that Rafael, somewhat ill at ease, kept his distance. There it was again, that elusive, never completely forgotten barrier. They attended the same pilgrimage, they drank the same wine, together sang the same songs but "we and they" were never forgotten, the two never really mixed.

The gut-vibrant, obsessive, primitive drumbeat had started up again together with the harsh, shrill flute. The slow martial tones created an unpleasant contrast to the fast, gay *rociero* songs, accompanied by hand-clapping or guitar, or with the stirring *Cante Hondo* with the fluid oriental subtleties. The beating drums had something menacing about them and they kept going, unrelenting, drowning out everything else. Throughout the night the drums kept beating, building up a mood of mute violence. The somber, savage, monotonous throbbing caught me and enveloped me. It was like the threatening rumble of the enemy tank in the night in the path of which, still unknowing, you might be inexorably caught.

In counterpoint to the undisciplined merrymaking and the frenzy of enjoyment, the drumbeat in the night, accented by the strident reed flute, carried an enigmatic, bluntly antagonistic, insane warning. It sent my blood into fever. I had the visceral sensation that, as it aroused in me fear, anger, and guilt, and with it a terrible passion for hurting, it easily could panic the population into acts of savagery. It carried an apocalyptic

sense of doom. I felt stirring in me echoes of my heritage, of the other side of the Spanish soul they called *menosprecio de la vida,* the disdain for life, the amnesia induced by its terror, that only led to savagery. The lack of sleep may have contributed to my waking nightmares of the vicarious experience of the Spanish Civil War, and the hard-to-forget memories of torches burning in the night of Nuremberg when the moment finds its men.

Hundreds of horsemen galloped wildly through El Rocio. They ripped and roared through the night in one of the wildest weekends Spain could offer. Daylight brought back more cheerful impressions.

Many Gypsies had set up camp near us. Every day and by the hour, more Gypsies arrived. Relatives of Rafael had come by truck. They brought fresh lettuce for sale, provisions, soft drinks, and beer. Some, of course, just came for the fun. Antonio Garcia Martinez came from Huelva and Lucas Porras Suarez from Cordova. Several of Rafael's brothers came late one night in their Mercedes-Benz van. Barely settled, they managed to borrow some horses and rode off at a gallop. The wine was flowing and food was being constantly replenished. They danced and sang and laughed eighteen hours a day, hospitable and gay.

From the time we had left Sevilla, Rafael had grown in my esteem. Among his own people, and because of Pedro's friendship, he included me, he opened up like a flower; he was the most attentive and considerate of hosts. In Benacasón Pedro had said this was Rafael's party. He splurged not only in wine and food but with a constant uproar of singing and dancing, wit and charm. I could hardly remember this was the shabby, anonymous little tourist photographer I had first met and disliked. This Rafael was an entirely different man; and Pedro, for that matter, became every day more *agitanado,* as Señor Parra had said in slighting tone. I enjoyed their enjoyment of the moment and felt privileged to be a witness to it, and, mellow with Manzanilla, part of it. It was the warmth and generosity of their companionship that for me made the *romeria del Rocio* what it was.

At the outer fringe of our Gypsy bivouac, a *payo* family from Sevilla was enjoying a picnic. The chunky, middle-aged grand-mother, dressed in black, encouraged her seven-year-old granddaughter, who at first coyly refused, to dance Flamenco to the singing of some young boys in our section. The little *payo* girl danced superbly. Spontaneously, a circle formed around her and everybody contributed additional *musica de palma,* handclapping music. When she tired, the Spanish grandmother danced. In spite of her plumpness and her age, she danced lively and very well. A young Gypsy boy joined her and danced the male counterpart. Rafael joined them, inviting the seven-year-old to dance with him. It was all light and playful.

When they all tired, a little Gypsy girl perhaps five years old started dancing on the back of the truck that belonged to Antonio, the one from Huelva. She used it to advantage like a raised stage. The circle changed its formation to include the truck into its periphery. Inside the empty truck, in the shade, an older woman, presumably Antonio's wife, was cooking on a small, improvised stove. With her spoon she beat out a fast counterbeat. The skinny little five-year-old flung back her head and froze in the pose of a seasoned professional. For a few seconds, she stood there immobile and arrogant. She beat out the rhythm with one foot until, suddenly possessed by it, she drummed her feet in a furious *taconeo,* heel-stamping. Her straight, unformed childish body suddenly became womanly, torso arched and hips swaying. Her arms moved languidly while her feet beat madly and on her baby face appeared a look of fierce disdain. The girl who danced first was technically superior, but this little thing had the *duende* or *angel*; she had "soul." I thought she was one to watch grow over the next ten years.

Antonio Garcia Martinez, *el de Huelva,* beat his palms in double tempo. All joined in. *"Ola, Remedio,"* he called, coaxing and with an edge of pride. "Ola, woman, show them how Flamenco is really danced!" But Remedio, his wife, did not leave the simmering kettle of food she was stirring in the back of the truck. *"Ola, Remedio, por Dios y por amor de mi,"* for the sake of God and for the love of me, he challenged. She left the stove, directing another woman sitting inside to watch over it.

From the shade she emerged into the light

on the backside where a moment ago her little granddaughter had shown herself off on the improvised stage. The *musica de palma* beat with crackling enthusiasm. An older, rough-looking man, with his bare knuckles against the side of the truck, tapped out an intricate rhythm of his own. Remedio was a woman well past her prime and she was plainly dressed, a woman more concerned with feeding her large family than putting herself on display. Her face was as passive as her general appearance; but to please her husband she had come forward. The handclapping grew thunderous. Then suddenly she snapped her fingers in *pitos* and it sounded like the angry cracks of a whip. Her arms and hands moved with the sinuous beauty of a swan and the swiftness of a hawk. The contained tension grew. Antonio barked out encouragement: *"¡Arsa! ¡arsa! ¡sá-sa-sa! ¡sa-sa-sá! ¡Venga!"* The driving rhythmic accompaniment of handclapping, *palmadas*, the tapping of knuckles on the side of the truck, the stamping of feet and finger-snapping grew more intense still. Then she burst loose in an explosion of energy, into a climax of rage.

And suddenly it was over. She went back inside the truck, sat down on the low wicker stool, and took over her duty as a grandmother, that of feeding the hungry crowds. With an incurable tinge of romanticism, I wished I had seen her young and beautiful, but did it matter? With such a passion and vigor, who needed youth? Neither had she need of the contrivance of colorful scallopped dresses, with molded torso and the trail of peacock flounce of the theatrical stage.

In the sudden silence that followed her dancing, Antonio intoned a song in complete counterpoint. It was intended to show her his appreciation and pride. "She is a true Gypsy wife," he sang in husky, broken tones of the plaintive, meandering *carcelera,* prison song. "She is a true Gypsy wife waiting for me at the prison gate."

Singing was, for him, an inner necessity, like dancing and handclapping was for the others. They did not perform their art for money, but only when they were in the mood and their audience understood and appreciated what they were doing.

A young man with a round happy face and smiles in his eyes sang songs of unrequited love and others about love gone away. An emaciated youth, very dark-skinned and with a bony, angular face furiously beat out a staccato *faruca,* without any preliminary setting of mood. He danced with what almost amounted to cruelty and with absolute male conceit. Afterwards, he stood aside and resumed his brooding, melancholy look.

Word of our private *juerga* spread and more and more Gypsies came to share in it. They intuitively seemed to know what the others were going to do and were capable of amazingly subtle, and at the same time emphatic, changes of rhythms. The range and variety were unbelievably wide. Gay *Sevillanas* contrasted with dances expressing pride and anger and the intoxication of despair. Songs of jest, flamboyant ululations, alternated with endless preliminary ay-ay-ay like the defiant cry of a wounded animal at bay, with frantic, raucous hymns of woe and supplication. Some were sung *a palo seco,* without accompaniment, others with all the abundant flourish of guitar improvisations, *falsetas,* or boldly, sweeping, vibrant *rasgueados,* often independent of the song itself. The mad overflow of emotion was like the gushing of springs.

The following day we barely made the Sunday parade of horsemen in honor of the Virgin of El Rocío, followed by the formal mass. The mass was attended on horseback and only to kneel did men dismount. This and the later parade of the statue of the Virgin were the highpoints of the pilgrimage. Without presuming to speak for the others, I had to admit that for me, the climax, without intending disrespect to the Virgin of El Rocío, had occurred the night before, the night of the *Cale*; that, to use or paraphrase the traditional opening formula to the folktales of the nomadic *Rom,* was: *Andi kodi swuntsi, sumnakuni rat kai tshi sas tai kai shoha tshi mai ditshola.* . . . In the golden holiness of the night that never was and that will never be again. . . .

The houses of the *Hermandades* were boarded up for another year. The Andalus started their long trek home. The Gypsies moved on to other fairs. *La Virgen del Rocío,* profoundly loved in Spain, in a strange, wild way, was left behind in the solitude of the swamplands.

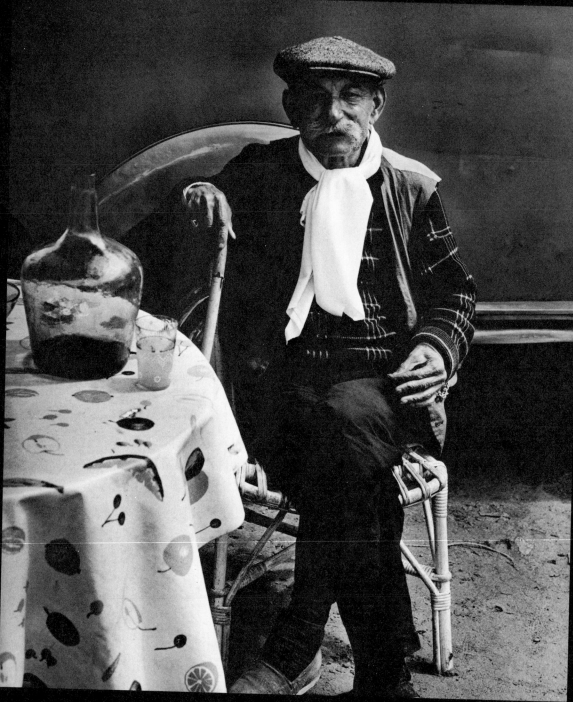

From all over Europe
the Gypsies come in the
spring to Les Santas
Marias de-la-Mare to
honor the uncanonized,
black Saint Sara.

Pagan in its realest sense, the festival, held at the end of winter, is a joyous welcome and renewal, a time for Gypsies to sing and dance their celebration of regeneration.

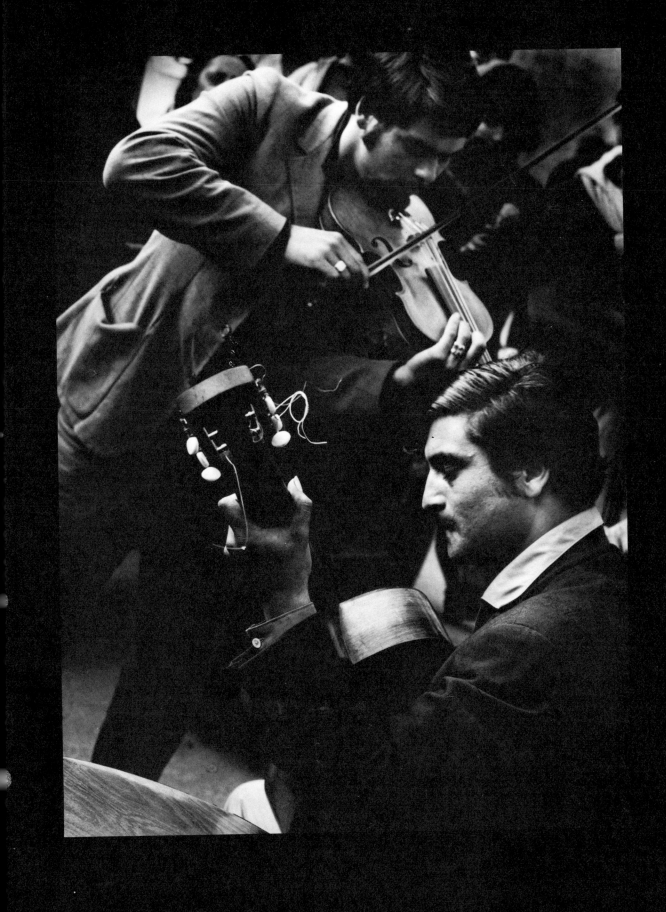

Chapter 12
Sevilla Again

Back in Sevilla, a last juerga at el Maestro. Cante Hondo building up to a shattering finale.

I WAS alone again, and in Sevilla, idling away a few days to rest and clean up from the red dust before leaving Spain. Making my airplane reservation had symbolically confirmed, with cruel finality, the turning of another page.

Pedro had gone back to the slums of La Chana and the *Cartuja.* Rafael had lingered on with fellow Gypsies. We had parted, numb with sleep, dizzy with sun, wine, and the sway of horse riding. Taking leave from them had come more easily than I had expected it would. After the many white nights of the *romeria,* saddle sore and insect bitten, I needed sleep and more sensible eating and drinking habits.

How natural it all had seemed yesterday, how remote and improbable already today.

The enchantment of Sevilla worked its magic and I indulged my more Sybaritic inclinations. The weather was at its best and I enjoyed long, quiet walks through the Barrio de Santa Cruz, deeply inhaling the fragrance of the last orange blossoms of the year, recollecting the events of the past few months here in Spain. I had not called on any friends I had made here and planned to spend this last day and night in complete privacy and rest.

In the early evening, after a relaxed *apertivo,* I regaled myself with some *angulas,* noodle-thin newborn eels served bubbling in peppery olive oil, prior to the usual Andalusian late, late dinner.

Crossing the Plazuela, that intimate, diminutive square in the old quarters, I heard a Flamenco guitar played as I had rarely heard before. Maybe it was due to the combined spell of the setting, the blue twilight, and knowing I was leaving all this behind in the morning. It all added up to that special charm of inaccessibility. I listened to the haunting, luxurious cross rhythms, the freedom and the fluidity of the playing. I let myself be mesmerized by its richness as it evoked the equally fluid, effervescent art of the Alhambra. With nothing in particular to do for the evening, I lingered on and soon found out that a *juerga* was taking place. Drawn like an insect to the candle flame, I discreetly slipped into the disreputable looking establishment, and overcoming my sensibilities and my upbringing, I invited myself. Although after El Rocio I should have been sated of *Hondo,* or at least my hunger for it satisfied, inexplicably I hungered for more. I realized the extent to which I had become an *aficionado.* I overcame my objections by rationalizing, indulging a further Andalusian hyperbole, that it amounted to a last meal before mounting the gallows.

A civil engineer from the copper mines near Huelva, on leave in Sevilla and on a spree, had thrown a party for a few friends. It already had been going on since the day before, and I had come upon it at its very tail end. The party was breaking up and there was some haggling about the amount of the musicians' fee. The *cantaor,* the guitarist, and several other Gypsies stood around talking when one of them stared hard at me. He briskly walked over to me. "You are the *rociero*, pilgrim to El Rocio. Is Rafael around?" We had met when Pedro had taken me to the Alcasar Bar looking for Rafael. I did not really remember him. "Let's have a *copita*, a drink," he invited, "maybe we can play and sing a little among ourselves." The offer was hard to resist but I promised myself, whatever happened, to keep an eye on the clock.

His nickname was *el Gato*, the cat, and he introduced me to the others descriptively as *el rocerio Hungaro de Rafael*, Rafael's nomadic Gypsy pilgrim. The *cantaor* was called *Tripas*, guts, and one of the others was *el Churi*, the knife. After a few more *copitas*, they said it was not safe to make music and sing after a certain hour, because of the *Guardia Civil*. *El Churi* invited us to his house a little outside the city.

On a wild impulse, I accepted. We hired a taxi and I invited the driver to be my guest at the *juerga* and to take me back to the city later. *El Churi* made it a point to argue about the price and settle on a mutually agreeable fee. We stopped after a fairly long ride, but instead of getting out, my new companions broke into a heated argument. Too late, it flashed through my mind I should have gone home and to bed. For my recklessness I deserved whatever trouble I was about to get into. Whatever happened now, it was too late for regrets.

El Gato wanted us to drive on to a different destination and he won over the others. Without consulting me, they explained to the driver where they wanted to go and how to get there. He looked at me and I nodded my confirmation. Instead of going to *el Churi*'s house, *el Gato* wanted to take me to the house of a "truly great *cantaor*" further out in the boondocks.

The night landscape under a great three-quarter moon looked unreal. The car stopped in an almost deserted spot. *El Gato* ran ahead to a hovel where the master lived *para*

areglar las cosas, to fix up things, meaning to arouse from their sleep the people who lived there and convince them to receive us. In the mood we all were in we had forgotten what time it was. *El Gato* came back within a few minutes saying: "They are waiting for us," which, under the circumstances, I appreciated as a rather ironic euphemism.

I was puzzled by, on the one hand, the deference *el Gato* showed our involuntary host and the way he addressed him as *el Maestro,* as did the others, and on the other hand his lack of consideration in rousing the old man out of his sleep at this hour for our pleasure.

El Maestro was a solid, squarely-built old man, with a face deeply etched by wrinkles and heavily pockmarked. He was casual and unpretentious. As if anticipating my concern, he told me that he no longer sang professionally and missed the *"ambiente."* He missed "his people," by which I realized he did not mean fellow Gypsies as much as "those of the *aficion.*" The *aficionados* were not primarily patrons or even enthusiasts, or, as some called them, addicts, but connoisseurs. *"¿Para quien quiero llorar si no tengo quien me oiga?* Why should I want to cry, if there is no one to hear me? We all need listeners more cultivated than ourselves," he said with the humility of the true artist, "in order to be able to give more of ourselves. And that is what we live for."

He made a gesture as if to invite us into the house, but it was clearly intended to invite protest. His family must be asleep inside. He took us to the back of the hovel and invited us to sit under the grape arbor. The night was light and clear and the temperature pleasant. From inside, a boy brought us a cold potato omelet, a bottle of wine, and some cherries.

The night grew lighter and I saw the pomegranate tree still lit by the moon and, beyond the thin, mastlike poplars, a thread of water, like molten glass, at the bottom of the riverbed.

El Maestro sat on a kitchen chair. "Sorrow either kills or makes one strong," he mused. His voice was hoarse as that of a crow. He carried on his soliloquy: "*Quien canta, sus males espanta,* with songs one exorcises one's demon"; after another slight pause, he added, "anyway there is no happiness, only happy men. . . ." The silence that followed seemed interminable.

El Maestro shifted his position and he sat at the edge of his chair. For a reason I could not fathom, the atmosphere was suddenly electrified, as if by a startling pause within the silence. I remember thinking, incongruously it seemed, and in contrast to the unbearable tension, that no domestic animal can sit as still as a wild one.

The old man, still seated, stamped his foot on the ground. His throat contracted as if to stop him, as if he had to force his words out between his teeth. For a second, I feared for him. Then unsolicited, with passion and vitality, he burst into a *soleá.* It was a magnificent song of solitude, deceptively simple and of intense spareness, the mute stomping of his foot the only accompaniment. His voice was broken and quavering and harsh but grew stronger and carried a deep sincerity. It was most unlike what, judging from his appearance, I had expected. *Tripas* leaned over to me and expressed in admiration that for which I found no words: "*que voz mas machuna de temple busco,* what a male voice of rugged fierceness." It had to the utmost what they called *eco Gitano,* or Gypsy echo, that quality uniquely theirs, harsh, wildly exuberant, throbbing with intense emotions. He sang with his whole body. His veins stood out and his throat quivered. *El Churi* and the others were in a total trance. The Spanish taxi driver was literally open-mouthed, and he had an almost demented glint in his eyes. *El Maestro* built up his mood from their reactions. It seemed as though the sound of his voice was accumulating in a confined space, like smoke gradually thickens and after a while makes the air almost suffocating—we were breathless from emotion and the mood of the moment.

With an abrupt change in time and rhythm, he then sang *siguiriyas,* building up to a shattering climax, only to resume stronger than before, building up with painful intensity toward another, and yet another climax.

He had a visionary look and I felt irresistibly seduced by the complexity of his emotion, by the persistence of his mysterious grief, deeper it seemed than the grief of all the others. He seemed to burn like a live coal, all earthiness gone. His slightly staring gaze seemed to look and perceive beyond visible things.

In the bluish light of the morning, my eyesight blurred by lack of sleep and tears, and even just a short distance away from him, it was impossible to tell if the tortured grin on his face was from anguish or ecstasy.

I was suddenly overcome by an urge, beyond all logic, and I heard myself say, "*Todo esta dicho,*" everything has been said, echoing my experience with Regalito and his brother, the nomadic horsedealers, when they, with these same words, and as was their privilege to do so, had broken off their singing. I meant to say that, for me, nothing more could be added.

El Maestro's gaze remained steady, but his eyes became hooded, implying an emotional disengagement. For a second, his mouth worked incoherently. Then he went on singing. I kissed his hand and walked away without turning back. His song followed me.

We drove back in complete silence, in time to pick up my luggage and make the plane to Madrid.

A few hours later, I left Spain.